TIME
TO
WAKE UP

THE COLLEGE STUDENT'S GUIDE TO OVERCOMING PRESSURE AND UNHEALTHY HABITS

LIZ WEI

For my parents. Thank you for everything you've taught me and for continuing to support me every day.

CONTENTS

Introduction

Alright, grab a pencil and a piece of paper. Ready?

Draw a tick mark if you've ever looked in the mirror and called yourself fat.

Draw a tick mark if you've ever sobbed in your room for multiple nights over a boy.

Draw a tick mark if you ever spent over 10 hours in a library wondering how you'll ever manage to learn the material on your finals.

Draw a tick mark if you've ever been upset because of your family.

Draw a tick mark if you've drifted from someone who used to be your rock.

How many tick marks do you have? I'll tell you mine – I have all five. Whether you have one, five, or your paper is blank, the following chapters are for you, sister.

Let me tell you a little about myself, just in case you're on the fence here about whether you actually want to read this or not. I graduated high school in 2017 and my god, I couldn't have been more ecstatic to get out.

You loved high school? I'm happy for you, genuinely. Senior year, however, was what I thought was the worst year of my life. My parents officially got divorced, kids in my accelerated learning program bullied me to the point where they drove to my house just to lay their hand on the horn for so long that my dog would cry, I had a huge fight with my best friend who I no longer speak to, you get the gist. On top of that, I went to a high school that wasn't in my town so I wasn't there when everyone decided who their lifelong friends were in elementary school. Darn.

The point here is that I didn't have many friends and I avoided going to class with those toxic (not all of them were toxic but the most vocal ones in the class were) people by hiding in my favorite teacher's room all day. I never said it out loud, but man I was depressed as anything.

That summer, I found the gym and birthed my passion for fitness. This passion helped me discover my identity. *I'm past the worst of it*, I thought. *I'm better now and I'm stronger now*, I thought.

You probably already guessed that I was wrong and if you did, you're correct.

Fast forward to the end of 2019. I hadn't been speaking to my dad in a month over an argument we had when I found out my mom had cancer in late November. I kept quiet about her illness, but her diagnosis scared the living crap out of me. When you find out someone you know has a mom with cancer you usually go, "poor (fill in the blank), that is just so sad". I mean, that's my initial reaction. Then one day I woke up and it was my reality too.

Universe, I know way more people than I should who have lost a parent to cancer and now you're telling me mine is sick too? Big yikes.

Anyway, two weeks after I found out about my mom, my dog died. Yep, at 6 AM on Thanksgiving morning my sweet angel of 15 years woke me up from a deep sleep with the most devastating sound I've ever heard. I heard a haunting cry coming from downstairs and moments later, she was gone forever.

Oh, but wait, there's more!

Three days later, my boyfriend broke up with me, out of the blue.

It doesn't end. A month after that, I had a big falling out with my best friends and they decided they no longer wanted to hang out with me anymore. That's pretty much all that has to be said about that.

That winter break I was even more depressed than I was in high school. My appetite subsided and every time I tried to go out with my friends and party to shake it off, it resulted in my calling my ex at 2 in the morning sobbing about how I hated my life and couldn't take another day of pain. Those were not my finest months… not my finest months at all.

I'm not asking for your pity here, trust me I pitied myself enough to last me my whole lifetime, I'm telling you all of this so before you begin to read, you can trust that whatever you're going through, I've probably been through it as well or something similar.

But look, here I am talking to you through a freaking book you just bought. Not only am I alive but I'm happy with myself.

I'm also telling you this so you can learn from my mistakes. I wrote this book based on habits that I didn't realize I was forming when I was so unhappy with myself. These habits created such a negative space for me and pushed me further away from being the person I wanted to be and reach the goals I had for myself.

The gym is my saving grace, it really is. It's transformed me into a stronger person inside and out and it's a great place to channel all my negative energy and turn it into something that was benefitting me, but what it didn't do is teach me what I'm about to teach you. That I had to learn myself, the hard way.
I've replaced all of those habits with new ones that I've formed that have changed my mindset, mental health, and physical health as well. I'm sure you've read a book like this before because I have, but I haven't seen one from a college student's perspective, so here's my best shot at it! It's time to wake up and start living every day.

Habit #1: Improving Yourself for Someone Else

"I don't care who I lose anymore, as long as I don't lose myself again, I'm good" – Unknown Author

Have you ever had your heart broken? I mean the don't get out of bed for months, think your world is ending, type of heartbroken. Yes? I feel your pain sister. No? I'm glad you've been spared the pain, but keep reading to minimize the heartache if it should happen to you somewhere down the line.

I had a few boyfriends in high school, but my first big girl relationship started at the end of the first semester of my sophomore year of college. This boy and I lived on the same floor freshman year and I swear, my heart actually leaped out of my chest every time he passed by me in the hallway, (especially the times he would walk past me with just a towel on).

I successfully sought out his Snapchat and began my pursuit to steal his heart. Months flew by, freshman year ended, and I was quite unsuccessful in my hunt other than the fact that we had a 90-day streak. Whoopee.

The day after Thanksgiving, our sophomore year, he asked me to his fraternity's date night which was the following weekend. This was completely out of the dang blue. I remember very clearly screaming out loud on my couch and then replying to him by saying, "yeah I'm down that sounds fun". I like to think I played that off pretty cool.

Although he was shy at first, I couldn't get over how freaking handsome this man was! I felt on cloud nine that I was actually going to be his date. What was everyone going to think on Snapchat? What was everyone going to think on Instagram? Will he post our picture? Is it weird if I post our picture? Will he even take a picture with me?

I could visualize telling our friends years from now how we met freshman year in Mettler Hall and the rest was happily ever after. Am I a little dramatic? Yes. Am I also a huge Disney nerd that still has a slight bit of hope I'll stumble across Prince Charming one day? Yes. The point is, I was over the moon ecstatic that I got to go to date night with this man.

The night of date night came and went and I had butterflies in my stomach the whole entire time. And yes, we did take a picture and we both posted it on Instagram. He asked to see me again and I spent my last days of the semester getting to know him more and more. The more time we spent together, the more I liked him.

By winter break, we were talking every day. If you've ever been in a relationship at school, I'm sure you know how it goes. We ended our nights together and slept in on the weekends, making breakfast for each other and walking across campus to get our favorite bubble tea. Heck we even went to Canada together!

As I said, I had one or two boyfriends in high school and no offense to them because they're lovely guys, but I didn't know what real love was until now. I looked forward to every time I got to see him and dreaded every goodbye, even though I knew it would only be a few hours or a day until I would see him again. I slept better when I was sleeping next to him, I woke up happier when I woke up next to him, and I had someone to walk me home every Saturday night at 2 am (and sometimes buy me a slice of pizza) so I never had to walk the Dirty Bruns alone. Sounds like a college girl's dream, right?

Well, there was this one big thing: he refused to call me his girlfriend. Emphasis on refuse.

I can't even count the number of times he watched me sob because he said he didn't want me to be his girlfriend, and then say he was sorry but that was his opinion. And every dang time it happened, I ended up accepting it. And that is on me, my friends, for letting it happen.

Before I knew it, sophomore year had already come to its close, and junior year was beginning. I met his parents, his cousin, we went to concerts together and snuck in burritos to the movie theater, the whole nine yards people. I am grateful for all of those memories for two reasons: the first one being that I was genuinely happy in those moments. The second is because I know now that everything we went through together was a learning experience.

You might be asking yourself, why the heck would you stay with a guy who so clearly did not want to be your boyfriend? Here's the simple answer: I stopped caring about myself and used all that energy to care for him instead.

I did everything in my control to be the best I could for him and prove that I was worthy of being his girlfriend.

Every time he was upset I was there for him with a shoulder to cry on. Every time he postponed our plans until nearly 12 AM because he wanted to "hang with the guys" I let him. Every time he had an invite-only party for his fraternity I knew better not to bother him with asking if he could get me a wristband so I would be let in (a wristband to be let into my own boyfriend's party … stupid I know, but I don't make the rules here), and ask his friends for one instead.

I let him curse at me and scream at me every time we fought. When I told him I really wanted to go see Thomas Rhett, he told me he wasn't interested and went with his friends instead and I kept silent on the matter. I didn't voice my opinion so he didn't realize he had hurt me because I didn't want to make a fuss and get into a fight. We never danced together at parties because he didn't want to. I didn't even bother him at parties because every time he was with his friends I was invisible. I wouldn't dare hold his hand in front of them either.

I cried and cried and cried but I let this all slide no matter how many times snotty tissues I had to throw out and finally in the fall he referred to me as his girlfriend! My heart soared! My work had paid off!

Things did not get better after he finally succumbed to using a title. Our arguments continued. I wanted to spend more quality time with him and he wanted to spend more quality time with his friends and his family, and I came second to that.

Before I continue, I should mention that my ex is not a bad man with some dark twisted soul. As a matter of fact, if he's reading this I want him to know I am thankful for our experience together because it taught me a lot. The fact of the matter is that he was in no way, shape, or form ready for a girlfriend and I pushed it on him by trying to be my best I could for him and prove him wrong. He knew he wasn't ready for a girlfriend but I had fallen in love and I would've done anything to keep him in my life. Because of that, we argued all the time. I sobbed my eyes out like it was my part-time job and he cursed his head off like it was the only words he knew. It was completely and horrifically toxic but my love for myself was too far gone to realize it.

Thanksgiving of 2019, my dog died. If you know me, you know my precious angel Maxie was my best friend in the entire world. She came home to us when I was in kindergarten and we've grown and been through everything together. She always knew how to put a smile on my face. To say the least, I was absolutely devastated when she passed.

With my heart holding on my threads, that Sunday of Thanksgiving break, before heading back to school, I asked my now boyfriend if I could stay over. I didn't want to be alone. I could barely sleep at night even after taking a Benadryl.

His response? Well, he said no because he wanted to do push-ups and homework in his room. I swear to you, my face actually turned red with anger.

I persisted and said, "Please can I just come over when you're about to go to bed? Just so I don't have to sleep alone?"

No.

"But you can do your homework and all that I just want to come over when you're going to sleep"

No.

I should also mention, he did not call me once after I told him my dog died. Not. Once. He apologized, but it still hurt for a long time after. Sad, mad and filled with every other toxic and terrible emotion, I stormed down the street to his house (yes, he lived one block over), when we got back to school and unleashed my rage.

I was done bottling up my anger. He had made me more that furious and I wouldn't stand for it! Was it a little crazy to show up to his door? Maybe a little, but he wasn't ignoring his phone and my armpits start to sweat when I'm mad okay. I'm also a firm believer that arguments should be done face to face instead of hiding behind a phone where things can easily get out of hand.

When I showed up and explained why I was upset, his response was, "I don't think we should date anymore".

I could've sworn my heart actually, physically shattered into a thousand pieces in that moment but the fact that I'm alive and breathing today to be writing this to you is proof that it in fact did not.

I'll spare you the details of my ugly crying (in front of his housemates, so embarrassing), and have you know that our relationship had hit its permanent dead-end that night and months of self-pity and depression followed.

Why was I so depressed after our break-up? There are two reasons. The first one is that I was also going through the death of my pup and finding out my mom had cancer at the same time. The second is because I had lost myself trying to impress him so when he was gone, I had nothing.

The key takeaway from this story is not that I wasn't treated the way I was supposed to be. The point is that I lost self-respect for myself trying to be what I thought he wanted me to be.

I got all dressed up so his friends would see me at parties and think wow he really got himself a pretty girl. I cried in my room every time he would push back our plans and when he said sorry I said it was okay because I feared losing him and I wanted to prove to him that I wouldn't be a nuisance if I was his real girlfriend. And that's why when he broke my heart three days after my dog died, my whole world collapsed.

Never once during this time did he ask me to look a certain way (unless you count when I asked his advice on what to wear to a fall-themed party and he told me I should look "fallesque", which is not a word but made me laugh). Never once did he ask me to act a certain way at a party or to his friends. I did this myself.

I am not proud of the person I was during our relationship and most definitely not for the few months that followed after it was over. I'll admit it – I acted totally, one hundred percent crazy-town when I got dumped. In my defense, I was dealing with a whole bunch of other crap. But that doesn't excuse my level of looney-bin.

My world crashed when he walked out because I had lost myself and was living for him. When he was gone, I had no idea what to live for. I used to tell him things like "you make me want to be a better person" or "you make me want to be stronger physically" not seeing the issues in those sentences.

Sure, I can motivate myself to go to the gym every day and get 4.0's but when it came to everything else, it all came back to what he would think and that's just how I thought relationships were and how it is when you're in love. So, now that you know my epic failure at a love story, here's my tip for you.

Improvement #1: Be Your Own Motivation

After a few months, my head finally emerged from underwater, and I was able to see why I went through what I did. That relationship taught me what to avoid in a man and how much I deserve. It also taught me not to lose sight of my own voice.

Once I accepted it was over, I started living for myself. My progress in the gym improved because I was more focused on my personal growth. I started writing workout plans and built my own website, breaking my first $1000 in profit only 3 months later. My Instagram following grew and I became a lululemon affiliate.

I began to take each day as a new opportunity to improve myself and ended each day by writing down five things that I love about myself and my life. When I started doing this is when things really took off for me.

Before this shift in mindset, I would've used my sessions in the gym to prove to him or my "haters" that I was much better than they thought I was, kind of like a "look at me now" slap in the face. Now, my sessions in the gym are purely for me. They are so I wake up every day and go damn Liz, you look great! They are so when I go to the beach I'm not self-conscious of my midsection in a bikini.

You don't need anyone to tell you you're special or worth it. The only person who needs to tell yourself that is you.

I could go on and on but you get the point. That whole, "haters are my motivators" phrase is complete crap. Yep, I said it.

Do you know what that phrase is? Bitterness, and the feeling that you need to prove your worth to other people.

Be your own motivation.

Let me repeat that just in case it didn't sink in, be your own motivation. I know it sounds cheesy, but focusing on what you think of yourself and on your personal growth will bring you much more joy than focusing on what others think of you. If you love yourself, it doesn't matter who doesn't love you. Let them fall back while you rise up.

Since I started focusing on my personal growth I've not only seen a change in my income and my social media following, but I noticed a difference in how I viewed each day. If you asked me January of 2020, I would've told you every day was another day of trying to survive hell. If you ask me now, I'll tell you that I am blessed to be able to live each day and take time to make myself a better version of myself. Since focusing on my personal growth, I have been the happiest about my body and my mindset than I can ever remember being.

Sure, there are people who inspire me. Seeing Whitney Simmon's posts? That inspires me but she is not my motivation, she is my inspiration. There's a fine line here.

It's hard to listen to this advice if you haven't already gone through something similar, trust me I get it. Remember how I said my ex isn't a bad person? He wasn't a great boyfriend, and he knows that, but I really mean it when I say he is not a bad person. In fact, he was the first one to tell me that I needed to learn to love myself before I could love anyone else. I remember getting so frustrated when he said that. I thought, I already go to the gym every day to make myself happy and I have great friends, I'm 20 years old I think I know how to make myself happy, sir.

And then I woke up. I realized what he meant.

I was not living for myself at all, I was living for him and he had recognized what was happening while I did not. And I thank God from the bottom of my heart for giving me my time with him to make me realize how important it is to live for yourself.

If my relationship sounds like yours, I encourage you to take a step back and make a list of the good and the bad in your relationship. It's so easy to make excuses for a person when you're in love. I was always the type of girl who swore I would never let a guy change me and I really believed that I wasn't letting it happen. Boy, was I wrong.

When you start living to make someone else happy or someone else's life easier, it's easy to become blind and biased to the way they act. You make excuses for their behaviors and tell yourself there is more good than there is bad. If the bad outweighs the good, or if you find that you spend more time trying to be better for him than for yourself, it's time to walk away sister.

Maybe he'll change and realize he can't lose you, or maybe that will just be the end and you'll know better for next time. My relationship was mentally abusive. Half of it was the way he treated me but the other half was because I let him. We were both at fault and I accept full responsibility for my end. It took me a while to accept it but I have now and it's brought me peace.

When you're living for yourself it's easier to stay in line with your boundaries and recognize what is good and bad for you. And it's okay if you've messed up, maybe you've been in a rut for multiple months like I was. The beautiful thing about life is that every day is a new opportunity to initiate change and hopefully now that you've read this, you'll become your own motivation and your own reason to be the best version of yourself.

Habit #2: Complaining About Things I Wasn't Working on Changing

"Fairytales can come true. You have to make them happen, it all depends on you" – Tiana, the Princess and the Frog

How many times have you looked at yourself in the mirror in the morning and said, "I look fat", then proceeded to spend the rest of the day lounging in bed watching Netflix and binging on whatever snacks were laying around the house?

For years, this is how I lived. I was unhappy with my body image and felt so uncomfortable when I had to wear a bathing suit because of the pouch that hung out at the bottom of my belly. My whole entire family had gym memberships but the more my parents pushed me to utilize my membership instead of "wasting their money" (okay so maybe I was), the more I refused to go.

Here's the key problem with that type of behavior: watching Netflix and snacking on whatever or how much you please won't make you shed some body fat or gain muscle. It has absolutely zero positive impact on your body.

Shocking, I know, but it's true. I resonate with girls who work hard on their bodies and their body transformations occur very slowly. Change happens with consistency but it happens at different rates for everyone. Change is also very rapid at first and then becomes more gradual. If you're working your butt off and hitting your macros every day, then by all means rant about your process sister! But if you're unhappy with your body image, or even your grades let's say, and you're not doing anything to change it… Houston, we have a problem.

My senior year of high school was more unpleasant than not. It had its ups, but it mostly had its downs. On top of pressure and bullying from my peers, I struggled with my body image pretty badly. I only wore high waisted jeans so it could suck up the bottom of my stomach, which by the way are very uncomfortable to sit in through an eight-hour school day and induce many, many cramps.

I compared myself to *everyone,* and especially to my tinier friends. One of my really close friends at the time was naturally thin. She could eat whatever she wanted and made about just as many trips to the gym as I did (which totaled zero) but her natural body fat percentage was just a lot lower than mine, which was hard for me to understand. We'd eat the same meals at Surf Taco but I would look three months pregnant after and she would look fresh off a runway. We have this one picture at the beach together and even though we're balancing on the rocks of the Manasquan Inlet with the Atlantic shimmering behind us, all I could see was how gigantic my stomach looked compared to hers.

Comparing your body to your peers can be extremely detrimental to your mental health. Everyone was skinnier or had a bigger butt or bigger boobs or nicer hair, from my perspective. There are still times today that I'm critical of my body. I wish my glutes would grow faster and I wish my body would shed fat faster, but I find comfort in the fact that every day I'm doing the best I can to fix these things. And the best I can is all I can do.

To be honest, there's always going to be that girl who is skinnier or has bigger boobs than you, that's just life. Part of it is genetics and part of it can be shaped by exercise and a healthy diet. But sitting around and complaining about your body while you shove your mouth with Doritos after school is not going to make it better.

All that time I spent complaining and comparing myself to others, that is essentially what I was doing – shoving my mouth with Doritos after school. Specifically, I was shoving my mouth with cool ranch Doritos. Let me be clear, I never had a problem with over or under eating. My relationship with food fortunately never border lined or became and eating disorder. I just had a great appreciation for junk food and no concept of how to have a healthy and sustainable diet. Nor did I care to change my eating habits for that matter. And that is exactly where my problem was.

I sat around complaining about myself and hating my body but I wasn't doing anything to help myself either. Instead I would come home and search the fridge for what ice cream was left that my brother and I hadn't devoured the day before. And on a nice day, I would top it off with some double stuffed Oreos or maybe some sour cream and onion chips. So, did I have the right to complain and be upset? No, to be quite frank I did not. In hindsight, I shouldn't have been shocked with how my body looked based on what I fed it.

Here's another example for you: have you ever felt completely overwhelmed by the amount of school work you have? If you haven't, what school do you go to … I'm just asking for a friend.

On a serious note, it's really easy to get overwhelmed with balancing school work and a social life in college, and I'll talk about that more later on. But before I do, let me ask you how much time you spend doing homework during the day versus how much time you spend on Instagram or Snapchat during the day. Let me also ask, when is the first time you pick up a book to study every day?

I've heard countless complaints from my friends and peers at school about how they pulled yet another all-nighter writing an essay or finishing an accounting assignment (those suck, by the way), but during the day I see them post that they were sitting at Starbucks all afternoon or talk about how nice their three-hour nap was.

Taking a trip to Starbucks is a great study break idea, but it's not a study break if you haven't started studying yet, sister. My response to those complaints is always, "well how much homework could you have gotten done if you hadn't taken a three-hour nap?" and most of the time, they answer with an excuse. Not a reason, an excuse.

If you're going to spend the day time watching TV, scrolling through social media, or getting lunch with friends, then you can't complain or be surprised when you're overwhelmed with school work that you haven't bothered to start, come 8 PM. This may sound harsh, but you're doing it to yourself girlfriend.

Some majors are harder than others and distribute more work, I totally get that! If you're maximizing your time and you're still feeling overwhelmed then let it out sister, vent! One of my housemates, Steph, spends the majority of the free time she has studying, so when she comes to me with complaints about school I listen openly because I know how hard she works for her grades every single day.

College is not easy! But if you're spending the day time sleeping or relaxing, recognize that you're digging yourself into your own hole and when it's time to crack open the books, you're going to be drowning in pages.

What about when we feel sad? What about when something bad happens to us that we need to vent about, something that's out of our control? Can we complain then?

With all of this being said, it's important to note there is also a time to be sad. Look, crappy things in life happens. Sometimes we lose family members, or we go through breakups or we get laid off from jobs and it is okay to be sad. It is one hundred percent okay to let your emotions out instead of bottling them up. But once they're out, it's time to sweep them up into the dust pan, throw them in the trash, and let the garbage truck pick it up from there.

In other words, there comes a point where it's time to move on. The only way we can move on from these situations is to work to pick ourselves back up, otherwise we'll be drowning in our sorrows forever. Ask yourself what you can do to help alleviate some of the pain you're feeling. Just like the trash bag said, "Don't get mad! Get Glad!". Cheesy again I know, but it's true. Doing what you can to fix or help the crappy situation might not actually resolve it completely, but at least you did what was in your power.

You probably get the point by now: you don't have the right to complain about things you're not working to fix, right? Here's what you can do to change your mindset and eliminate things to complain about.

Improvement #2: Consistently Work to Change What You're Unhappy About

Change will not happen on its own.

Jiminy Cricket tells us that when we wish upon a star, anything our heart desires will come to us. What he doesn't mention is that in addition to wishing, we must take action towards our dreams to make them happen.

I believe Disney corrected themselves there when they created Tiana from the Princess and the Frog. You know how the song goes, fairytales can come true but you have to make them happen, it all depends on you! I make a lot of Disney references, just an FYI.

Tiana's daddy was right when he told her that. You have to work hard to reach your goals or to change what you're unhappy about.

Let's go back to my struggles with body image.

I am a NASM certified personal trainer. I also run an Instagram account to share my workouts and advice to inspire others. I think I get called "Lifts with Liz" more than I get called just Liz these days – no complaints.

As you probably already guessed, I wasn't always so passionate about fitness. I wasn't born with loads of muscle. I had to start somewhere. That summer after high school graduation, I made a commitment to myself to start going to the gym regularly. I realized that no matter how many times I looked at myself in the mirror, that wasn't going to fix what I looked like each time I waddled up to it.

Complaining about my body wasn't going to give me prominent ab muscles or shed body fat. What is was going to do was continue to destroy my self image and annoy those around me that I constantly complained to.

I chose to ignite change. Since that summer I have gone to the gym six days a week and learned how to properly feed by body to fit my goals. I fell so in love with my transformations and how powerful it felt to be a strong woman that I pursued and achieved my personal training certification.

What I love about personal training is that each client is there because they are igniting their own change. At some point they decided to pursue getting stronger or learning shedding off fat and decided to get a personal trainer and I praise each one of them for showing up and putting in the work. It's a bonus for me that I get to help them achieve their goals.

My point is that at some point I quit sitting on my butt and complaining. Instead, I used what I was unhappy about to motivate myself to make a change. See how I tied that back into improvement number one?

Like I said, there are still days where I think I look a little fluffy or I wish my glutes were bigger, but the difference now is that I am actively making a change about these flaws I see in myself – instead of doing jack squat, I'm doing back squats (bad joke, I know).

How about school work?

Well, stop taking three-hour dang long naps!

If you're feeling overwhelmed with the work you have, start recognizing how you can be using your time differently and change the way you currently run your homework routine. If you skip the three-hour nap to finish your homework, it means you can spend the time you would be finishing those assignments at 12:30 AM sleeping instead. Getting a good night's sleep eliminates the need for that mid-day nap!

You know how when you learn about addictions in high school health, they tell you the first step in recovery is recognizing you have a problem? The same thing can be applied here. Recognizing how you waste your time can help you make adjustments in your schedule to use time more wisely and hopefully eliminate some of the stress college throws our way.

One of my closest friend's is a girl named Abbey. One day while we were texting, she told me one day that she was going to start calling me Ms. Complainer because I complained so much. I know that everything Abbey says is out of her want for me to a better version of myself, so I reflected on what she said instead of getting offended by it.

My friends, she is not wrong. I did complain *a lot* and knowing Abbey, she wouldn't have minded if it was about serious things because when I do come to her with those tears she whole-heartedly listens.

It was the complaints about nonsense that I wasn't working to fix that made her say that. It was the little things like, "my brother always leaves his beard shavings in the sink and it's so gross" that I would say to her. The catch is that I would never tell my brother to please stop leaving his shavings in the bathroom sink.

No matter how trivial the complaint is, before it leaves your mouth ask yourself if you've done anything in the past 24 hours to try and change what you're complaining about. If the answer is yes, let it out. If the answer is no, swallow those words and use them to ignite change.

CH. 3

Habit #3: Blaming My Failures on Others

"I've learned from the pain and turned out amazing" – Ariana Grande

I don't know about you, but I'm a Taurus and so by nature, I'm stubborn as anything. I don't know much about astrology but I know that Taurus' are supposed to be stubborn and that one fits the shoe perfect so I guess this stuff isn't total B.S.
One of my biggest flaws is that I hate admitting when I've done something wrong. This goes for falling outs with friends, arguing with my mother, and even my own physical and mental progress.

Part of what made me fall so in love with weight lifting was the progress I was seeing and the way it made me feel. The gym became my outlet to release all of my negative energy and anxious feelings. Over the first year of my fitness journey I saw my body transform to put on more muscle in my upper body and even in my legs a little, which I always struggled with. Despite all the progress and I'd made, one thing I didn't see was a change in my body fat.

As I mentioned before, my body fat was one of my biggest insecurities. I was never actually overweight but sadly, all my fat naturally deposits right to my stomach. Like a lot of girls, my stomach is something that I've always been hyperaware of.

I spent the next two years, two full years, continuing to judge myself in the mirror and rant to my friends (and that ex-boyfriend I mentioned earlier), about my body fat. Why aren't I seeing change? Am I destined to be fat because of my genetics? Do I have to stop eating pasta altogether or something? I really don't want to have to give up pasta…

At this point in my life, I was actually doing something about my physique and physical health as opposed to the stage in my life I talked about in the last chapter, where the only thing I was doing for my body was feeding it with high-fructose corn syrup.

At this point I had regularly been going to the gym six days a week. My frustration stirred as I continued to exercise but my midsection remained the same.

I blamed my birth control.

I blamed my genetics.

I blamed Brower Commons (the crappy dining hall at Rutgers).

I blamed the female body's ability to expand in order to reproduce.

I blamed every possible excuse I could find on the internet instead of taking a step back and looking at my habits, or taking the time to read some material or studies behind "cutting" to understand how the fat loss process works.

Might I add that I was all too aware of the great pain and unpleasantness cardiovascular exercise brought me so I rarely chose to work any form of it into my exercise routine, other than the stationary bike. The stationary bike is the least breathtaking form of cardio, it just is.

At the time, I thought that because I ate what I considered to be healthy foods that I should've been shedding weight like a layered-up wrestler in the sauna.

I ate eggs and an English muffin for breakfast. I ate a salad for lunch and dinner. I had protein shakes and protein bars. Why was I not seeing any change?

I had this belief that if you ate clean (or cleanish) foods then you would just automatically be skinny. I thought, okay I'll snack on almonds after dinner because nuts are healthy, and after dinner I would proceed to finish half a container of Blue Diamond almonds. The toasted coconut ones are like crack. Well, I don't actually know what crack is like but I assume that they are the almond equivalent.

Did you know that that one gram of fat contains 9 calories, whereas protein and carbs are 4 calories? Did you know that nuts, almonds included, are very fat heavy foods and therefore very caloric? Pre-personal trainer Liz did not.

I'll let you in on a little secret here: you can eat as clean as you want but if you're consistently overeating, you're not going to lose weight.

Until I had bought a food scale, which I'll talk about in a bit, I had no idea about the amount of food and calories that I was eating!

The point I'm trying to make here is that I blamed everything else but myself for my failures. I never considered taking a step back and doing some self-reflection along with a few google searches to understand my mistakes and make improvements from there on out.

Put yourself in this situation.

You get to college and make a new best friend. Quickly, this girl becomes your rock, your go-to, your dance partner, your hold the door while I squat in a frat house bathroom girl. You get it.

Over time, you tell each other your deepest secrets and you wipe each other's tears. Every heartbreak one feels, the other one feels too. It's no question to you that this girl is going to be your bridesmaid one day at your wedding.

You think to yourself, this is what college is all about. College is about finding those true friends that will last you a lifetime. Years from now your kids will call her Aunt and you'll sit back and think about the days you used to hold each other's hair back and finish each other's pizza in the wee hours of the morning.

And then one day, you get into a fight.

I'm not talking a little argument, I mean a friendship-ending fight. The killer part: you never saw it coming.

One day, out of the complete freakin blue, she sits you down and tells you that you haven't been a good friend to her. She feels like you've put her in awkward positions and sometimes she's scared to talk to you about things because your tough love comes across more tough than it does love, apparently. In fact, she tells you that you've never really done anything for her.

Confusion and memories rush to your head. But what about the time you kept that big secret for her? What about the time you lied to her mom about her whereabouts to cover for her? What about the time you got her coffee because she was sad? There's no way that she could possibly be serious!

At this moment, you have two choices. You can listen and reflect on what your friend is saying to you or you can twist the blame and put it on her,

You can tell her she's overreacting. You can make a list of all the things you've done for her and all the secrets you've kept. You can tell her that she took everything the wrong way because you never meant to hurt anyone, you don't even have a mean bone in your body!

What I'm about to say next is very important to remember: if someone tells you that you've made he/her feel a certain way, that means you did something to make he/her feel like that. You might not have meant it, you might be completely shocked by this, but the cold, hard truth is that something you did made the person feel this way.

More often than not, it's a misinterpretation. The learning part of this is now you know that what you said/did is easily misinterpreted and next time you'll act more carefully.

If you choose to turn the blame on her, I can assure you matters will only get worse.

Improvement #3: Practice Self-Reflection Often

You might've guessed that I went through something pretty similar. If you did, give yourself a little pat on the back for excellent foreshadowing skills!

Luckily for me, I still had some other friends left after this incident. Abbey, who I mentioned earlier, was one of them. Abbey is the type of person you run to when you need advice because she's just so dang good at it. When I came crying to her, she told me to suck it up and apologize. She told me to swallow my pride and understand what Leila was upset about, rather than argue back with her that she was wrong and prove to her that I was in fact a great friend.

So, that's what I did.

I took every word my friend had said and before answering, I opened my journal and started writing down the things she found wrong on my end of our friendship.

I took the time before responding to understand how my intentions could've been blurred and how I had hurt her feelings or put her in uncomfortable situations numerous times throughout our friendship. When I was done with my self-reflection, I apologized.

I didn't blame her for misunderstanding. I didn't try and explain how she was wrong and make her see differently. I took her words and I apologized for my wrongs.

I wish there was a happier ending to the story but she accepted the apology and stood her ground on her decision that she no longer wanted to hang out with me.

You might be asking yourself, okay Liz so you followed this "advice" you're trying to give me and it didn't fix your friendship, so why on earth should I follow it?

It brought me peace. Peace with yourself is such a gratifying feeling. Knowing I did the best I could and swallowed my pride to try and make things right is satisfying to me. I did the best I could. It didn't work, but I did what I could. I didn't say anything nasty back that she could hold against me, I didn't fight her or blame her for ruining our friendship, I accepted that I had failed her and learned from my mistakes.

Self-reflection, when done right, will open your eyes to your wrongs and show you how to move forward next time. I might have lost a friend but I learned from the experience and figured out ways to improve myself.

As for my weight loss dilemma, I quit blaming external factors and cracked down on myself and my habits, I became educated on how to feed your body according to your goals and May 2019 I began my first serious cut.

I am fortunate enough to be disciplined in a sense where tracking my macros and weighing my food is not unhealthy for me, mentally. I realized that if I was serious about wanting to cut my body fat, I was going to have to become serious with how I was feeding myself. If I was going to track my food, it meant I had to stop sneaking in one or two pretzels every couple of hours and not tracking it. It meant if I was going to have ice cream I had to save room for it and maybe have a smaller dinner.

When I stopped blaming other things and blamed my own habits, I started to see change.

That summer my body fat dropped from nearly 26% to 22%, the lowest my body fat had ever been. For the first time in life I was starting to see definition in my stomach and I felt comfortable going to the gym in a sports bra and leggings (and now I can't go back to wearing sleeves in the gym ever again, I just can't).

All this time that I thought my genetics were holding me back because I was built to be a bit wider like my dad, I was just making excuses for myself instead of implementing change.

There are times where other people are going to wrong you. There are times where external factors will come into play that you can't control. But in every situation, it's a great practice to self-reflect and ask yourself if you had a role in what went wrong. Sometimes you won't, sometimes you will but you won't know if you never take the time to put aside your pride and ask yourself if it's a possibility.

This whole book essentially is on self-improvement and how to become a better version of yourself. Being able to recognize your flaws and learn from your mistakes is the biggest way we can start improving ourselves every day.

Habit #4: Steering from My Path

"People often ask me if I know the secret to success and if I could tell others how to make their dreams come true. My answer is, you do it by working" – Walt Disney

Now I know I don't speak for everybody when I say this but… I hate doing homework. I hate it.

I hate Wiley Plus. I hate writing business proposals. I hate Pearson Learning. I hate all of it. Homework is so incredibly boring and most of the time (and now I'm not entirely sure I should be saying this), it's on Quizlet anyway if you look hard enough.

With that being said, I get it done. Not only do I get it done, but I get it done early and at least a day before the submission date.

I was never the type of person to regularly turn in late homework, or at all for that matter, but I am someone who has constantly felt overwhelmed and incredibly bored by the amount of homework I've been assigned in college.

There're a million things under the New Brunswick sun that I rather do than sit down and compose a Marketing Research data analysis, so I would do them.

Exam on Monday? Let's go to Tacoria on Sunday night.

Accounting homework is due at midnight? I think I'm going to spend an extra hour in the gym.

Paper is due by the weekend? Well, I can't possibly start it now, I'm too busy watching Raini Rodriguez videos on YouTube with my housemates (erm, don't ask how we stumbled upon these but if you choose to look them up thank me later, no offense Raini), and then we're getting ice cream later.

Oh, and did I mention it's a gameday tomorrow?

Needless to say, obligations are something we as people tend to avoid and put off because it's not something we want to do, it's something we have to do.

I have no problem getting myself up at 8 AM every morning to get to the gym before class because working out is my favorite part of the day. However, if you asked me to get up at 8 AM to work on a group project, there's no way in heck I would get out of bed for that.

Because of this, it's easy for me to distract myself with things I find much more interesting, therefore putting off the things I need to get done.

I mean guys, I can't even do my homework in my room anymore because I have a big mirror on my desk and I will sit there plucking my eyebrows instead of studying. Seriously, look at my eyebrows there is never a hair out of place.

How many times have you told yourself you want a 4.0 GPA or to make the Dean's List? But then how many times have you participated in other activities, such as partying in Pike's basement until the wee hours of the morning on a Saturday when you have an organic chemistry exam Sunday night?

There needs to be a balance between social life and academics.

Read that again: balance.

That means not letting your schoolwork take over to the point you neglect your friends. That also means preventing your social life from negatively affecting your GPA.

How many times have you started a new workout plan or told yourself you were going to start eating healthy, but on Friday you found yourself elbows deep in a Chipotle Burrito with extra guac, please.

How many times have you told yourself that you were going to start a new job because you really wanted to make more money but then proceeded to quit because the hours were annoying or it turns out that fetching people extra sides of ranch dressing isn't really your thing?

How many times have you let yourself stray from the path you put yourself on?

College is one of the most exciting times we'll live through. There are so many campus activities to engage in and so many new people that we come across but it's also an incredible period of learning. We are given four (give or take a few depending on your situation) years to explore our interests and dive into our futures.

For some, this means landing an internship at a major corporation. For some, this means starting a small business. For some, this means getting promoted at their job. For some, this means learning a new trade that will become their career.

I am all about trial and error, I have failed more times than I've succeeded. But there is a difference between failing and taking a step back, and getting distracted and taking a step back.

We often go through inspirational periods where suddenly we have a million things that we won't accomplish. We wake up one day and try to set out for all of them. Before we know it, we're drained and end up sitting on the couch instead of hanging out with the girls just like any other day.

Pursuing your dreams doesn't sound that hard, right? It's when we have seven dreams at once that things become overwhelming. Have you ever tried to start eating healthy, spend a certain amount of time in the library, keep your room clean, and search for jobs all on the same day?

You probably started the day off right with a healthy breakfast but then ended up throwing clothes all over the place when you realize you're late to class now because you made breakfast. And then when you're at the library you realize you're going to be there longer than you thought to do some job searching, so you cave and make a trip to the vending machine and get yourself a bag of Lays and a medium hot coffee.

How do we avoid this crash and burn out from happening?

Improvement #4: Make a List of Your Priorities and Stick to Them.

Start by making a physical list.

I don't care if it's in your journal, on your mirror, or in the note's app on your phone. Make a list of what's important to you and prioritize them. This has helped me plan my days and figure out what I should be doing and what I can be doing with my time.

More often than not, we let ourselves stray from working towards our goals because it's easier or more enjoyable to engage in activities that aren't necessarily helping us. Sure, I would love to sit and watch All American on repeat all night but I have an essay to get to and I really want a 4.0 this semester. I would love to sleep in an extra hour in the mornings but I have body goals I promised myself I would work on so I get up and go to the gym.

My list includes my relationship with my family, my health, my academics, my social life, my income, and time to myself.

You might not agree with the order of my list but that's okay, that's why it's mine. Your priorities might come easy to you and if they do, that's great! For others, you might have to think for a little while. The important thing to remember is to set them in place.

From here, my list of priorities helps me decide how I'm going to spend my day. I am crazy about my health. Because of this, I make sure I get up each day with enough time to make myself breakfast and go to the gym. I also make sure there's time in my day to eat three balanced meals.

Ideally, I like to work out in the morning but sometimes with my school and class schedule, that's not realistic. So, what do I do? Carve out another hour in the day. Sometimes this means getting up an hour earlier or staying up an hour later to make sure I have time for a workout. I always get my workout in when I'm supposed to.

After my health, the next priority on my list is my academics. I have always been a school-oriented person and grades matter a lot to me. Sometimes this means I have to spend a Friday night in the library instead of partying with my friends or watching movies with my housemates. Most of the time when I tell someone this is my plan for the night I get the response, "you're lame" or "do you really have to study all night?".

Truth be told, my mental capacity reaches its limit at around 10 PM so it's enough time for me to go out anyway, but I don't leave the library until I have completed the tasks I needed to.

Sometimes I feel like my brain is going to implode right there in the middle of Alexander Library. I can't bear another second of studying. So, you know what I do? Pull out my list of priorities and remind myself why I'm here.

After my school work is done, I can go out and have my fun!

My income does not fall far behind my social life. I prioritize my social life over my income just because I am a firm believer that a life with no friends is not a life worth living. It doesn't matter if I only have two friends, I rather have two than have no one to create memories with and spread my love to. It's important for me to spend time with them and be there for them when they need me.

Success in all aspects comes with hard work.

I've been going to the gym religiously for three years now and I'm still working to get my body to where I want it to be, but I've put in hours of sweat and eliminated so much garbage (that I enjoyed) from my diet to improve my health and physique.

Spring semester of my sophomore year, I wanted a 4.0 so badly just to brag and say I got a 4.0. It's a pretty impressive statement and a real jaw-dropper. At that time, I was working an internship as well as my job at the gym, whilst also juggling my health and my social relationships.

Every Wednesday I would leave Rutgers at 8:30 AM to go back home where my internship is, work 9-5, come home and go straight to the gym where I would work for an hour as a personal trainer, and then finally get my own workout in. It doesn't stop there. After that I would grab a quick (and healthy) dinner from the dining hall and go straight to the library to study. Finally, when the moon was high in the sky I would pack my bags up and leave to go spend time with my then-boyfriend.

It was hard. It was mentally exhausting. I was constantly running around with multiple bags that were stuffed to the brim with everything I needed so I didn't have to waste time going home to reorganize and recollect.

However, I was never late to work, I ate lunch with my mom and my puppy twice a week on my lunch breaks, and I never missed a workout or homework assignment.

When I saw the 4.0 on my transcript at the end of the semester I practically leaped for joy. I did it! And my priorities helped to keep me on track.

There were so many other ways I could've spend my time outside of work and class but they would've been detrimental to goals, steering me away from the path I wanted to be on.

Start small. Start by writing what's important to you and then ordering it. Constantly remind yourself of these things every morning when you're starting your day. Remember it the next time you decide iced coffee is a sufficient breakfast because its quick and easy, or that going out to dinner is much more fun than studying for your exam.

Staying true to your priorities will help you achieve the things you set out for.

Habit #5: Giving Up on My Goals

"When you really want something, you'll find a way. When you don't really want something, you'll find an excuse" – Rachel Hollis

Put yourself in the following situation. It's a Saturday afternoon and you've decided to finally start cleaning your room (or dorm room). Halfway through cleaning, when there's clothes and books and perfumes you forgot about all over the floor, you just give up. You flop down on your bed and close your eyes. You decide, okay I actually don't want to do this anymore and I don't care if my room is a mess forever.

I'm guilty.

There have been countless times in my life where I've set out to do something and it never gets done.

I talked about straying from the path I want to be on but there have been countless times that I just took a different direction completely.

Sometimes it's little things I give up on like I want to start regularly practicing yoga or I'm going to cut tortilla chips out of my diet or even I want to make paintings to sell online. Sometimes it's big things like, I want to find a new job.

I am a dreamer.

I like to visualize myself doing all the things I want to do or being all the things I want to be. I set out for it. The problem is, I have a long list of things I'm interested in doing or what to improve and my ambition overwhelms me if I set out for all of those interests at once.

Is it really realistic to aim to be a yoga guru, a culinary star in the kitchen, start a small business and try a new diet (I use the term diet loosely because I'm a firm believer that diet fads are more harmful than they are helpful to your body), all at once?

It's not.

What ends up happening is I realize how hard it is to commit to one new thing, let alone try and commit to five new things. I end up getting extremely overwhelmed and drop the tasks all together. In other words, I give up on the goals I have for myself. After all, that is why we have our list of priorities. We focus on one thing and then go down the list. It's better to focus on one thing at a time and put all your heart into it than to put a fraction of your heart into many things at once.

Before my fitness journey came to what I officially recognize as it's beginning, I made some attempts at launching myself into a healthy lifestyle. The summer after my junior year of high school I made the occasional trip to the YMCA and would go on the elliptical or bike for three miles and call it a day.

I started going for two reasons. The first reason was that I was bored out of my mind and could now drive. The second reason was that I hated my body and thought that cardio was the answer to all my prayers (mind you, this was still in my junk food-loving stages of life). My ultimate goal was to use my free time to shed some body fat. You could call this a slow start but because I was so inconsistent with my gym routine, my workouts had no real value to me.

I soon realized that cardio is hard and painful and that the gym took up time away from tanning or reading or hanging out with my friends, so I stopped going.

What happened? My body didn't change. My physical health didn't change. I had given up on my goal and went on a completely different path than I wanted to be on – the path where I was still insecure with my body and not in the best shape I could be by any means.

I have friends that dream of starting their own podcasts or selling their own clothes or sharing their artwork with the world. But on top of school work, social life, and their other priorities, it never gets done. It's sad to see something that could've been so valuable to the world pushed so far under the bed but I understand why it does. It comes back to our list of priorities, friend. It also comes down to how much is on your plate at once.

I am constantly loading my plate to its max capacity and then coming back for a round of seconds. I mean this literally and metaphorically, you don't want to see me when dessert rolls around on Christmas.

What I mean for the purposes of what you're reading is that I always take on as much as I can. Part of it is because I feel capable and the other part if because I hate saying no.

When my boss asks me to come in and lead InBody exams at the gym (those assessments that tell you the breakdown of your body), I'll squeeze it in between classes, work, my workouts, and my time to study. I squeeze it in even if it means I skip out on my usual lunchtime. Why? Because I hate to say no to opportunity. When my dad asks me to get dinner right in the middle of my study time, I say yes and delay my studying by an hour because I hate saying no and I love getting poke with my dad.

What ends up happening every dang time is I try to be too many things at once – a good daughter, a good student, in control of my physical health, a good employee, etc. – that I end up losing sight of at least once of these things.

Another factor that leads me to give up on my goals is the fact that they are hard. I know, I talked about this a little last chapter but I'm bringing it up again because not only is it relevant to this topic but I feel as if this generation slacks when it comes into putting in the work.

So many things are handed to us these days or placed right in front of our faces. I know so many people who have never worked a real job in their life and it befuddles me how they could've gotten this far in life without having a job. I learned so much in the four years I spent wrapping burritos and making tacos.

I am a firm believer that you will get rewarded, in some way, for the work you put in. "Work" goes beyond how hard you study and how many hours are clocked in on your paycheck. Sometimes this means buying a suit so you have something to wear to the career fair or taking an hour out of your day to attend the lunch with EY that your school has set up.

My school gives its students so many opportunities to network with big-league professionals. They're constantly sending out emails that practically say, "Here! We are literally putting big four firm employees in front of your faces at this time and this place! Please come!" and most students won't go because it requires effort to get dressed and physically get themselves to wherever the meeting is.

Giving up on your goals doesn't always mean crinkling them up and Kobe-ing them into the nearest waste bin, never to be seen again. You give up on your goals every time you actively decide not to work towards them.

Improvement #5: Turn Goals into Habits, One at a Time

I often get asked, "how do you stay motivated to go to the gym every day?" or, "how do you find the time to go to the gym every day" and sometimes even, "how do you balance everything in your life?".

The truth is, sometimes I feel like I'm a juggling act, but most of the time I don't worry about what I can get done because I've created habits for myself. These habits are part of my routine.

A while ago, my goal was to improve my physique by losing body fat and building muscle. For years in school I learned about SMART goals and worked on what seemed like stupid and trivial exercises about making personal SMART goals. It seemed tedious and useless at the time but if you take a minute to understand what the SMART format is implying and forcing you to do, you'll realize it's a pretty helpful technique.

SMART stands for specific, measurable, achievable, realistic, and timely.

I could go into the specifics of how to create a smart goal, but that's already available on a hundred different sources on google. Instead, I'll tell you how I achieved mine.

Formatting your goals to fit the SMART format allows you to create almost an outline for your goals. It makes the goal specific and gives you a timeline and realistic ways to achieve this goal.

The next step after creating your goal is to manifest that goal and make it a habit.

When I get that question asking how I'm motivated and find time to go to the gym today, I answer by saying that it's part of my routine. My weekday schedule is very uniform from week to week every semester. I take a moment before the beginning of the semester, and sometimes at the end of each night, to ask myself: when do I have time to go to the gym tomorrow?

Sometimes this requires me to get up earlier and sometimes I'm able to fit it in midday or when my classes and work are over. It varies by day. Nonetheless, the time I go to the gym every day says the same each week. I know that 1:00 is my gym time on Mondays so if someone asks me to grab lunch then, I turn them down because I am busy at that time.

If you're serious about the goals you want to achieve, I can't stress enough how important it is to turn the actions that will help you achieve them into habits.

A couple of years ago I easily would've blown off the gym to go eat with my friends. Taking that path means I would've been actively choosing to not work on my fitness-oriented goal.

What I'm trying to say here is that if you really want to achieve something, you have to make time for it in your daily routine.

You make time for what is important to you.

Figure out what you need to do to achieve your goal. In my case, it was getting my butt to the gym six days a week to put in the work. After you find out what you need to do, carve out time in your schedule for it and stick to it every week. The way you wouldn't blow off your shift at work because you were, let's say, tired, you shouldn't blow off working towards your goals.

Before you start to make your goals into habits, pick one first.

There are a lot of things I'd like to achieve in my lifespan but as I mentioned earlier, it's easy to become overwhelmed when you set out for too many things at once. Don't get me wrong, ambition is such a powerful trait to possess but at some point, we have to know what our boundaries are and take a second to slow down. It doesn't mean you're never going to achieve said goal, you just might have to put that one on the back burner right now.

I decided to get my personal training certification at the beginning of the summer after my freshman year of college. At that time, there were a few other goals I had for myself as well. I wanted to own my own car and I wanted to learn how to cook healthy meals.

If I had set out to do all three at once, it would've been really hard finding time to study for my certification while working enough to find the money for a car, and then when would I have time to start learning how to cook on top of all of that?

I drew up a priorities list. Which one of these was the most important to me? Which one should I focus on first?

I decided to start with my obtaining my personal training certification. Becoming a personal trainer would open new windows of economic opportunity for me that I could use towards saving up for a car. And as for the kitchen? Well, my skillets and YouTube will always be there for me when I get around to that goal. I wasn't giving up on it, I was just saving it for when I had time to focus whole-heartedly on it.

I figured out what it would take to reach this goal of getting my certification. I bought a self-study course and signed up for an exam, giving myself a deadline. I made a goal of studying one chapter a week so I could finish the material by the end of the summer. The action I needed to take to reach this goal was studying. The next step is to make studying a habit that fits into my routine. I carved out time to study for at least an hour a day in my daily routine and stuck to it. By the end of the summer when it was time to take my exam, I had finished learning all the material and I passed. Woohoo!

After my certification was complete, it was time to start working my next goal into my routine - saving up enough money to buy a used car. A few months later, after working two jobs, I became the proud owner of a little gold Jetta (I do not have a name for her unfortunately but she is a she).

After all of that, I finally had time to learn how to cook. I began to meal prep for myself every weekend and I'm proud to say that my culinary skills have increased exponentially in the past year. I make a mean stuffed pepper.

If I had tried to complete all of these goals at once, I would've overwhelmed myself. I wouldn't have enough time between working and studying to eat let alone learn how to cook!

It took time. I had to push some things off to get other things done. However, in hindsight, each of those goals has been achieved. Pushing a goal off doesn't mean you're giving up on it, it just means you're saving it for when you have time to devote the attention to it that it needs.

Start small and create habits for yourself. Habits require discipline which will take you far in life.

Habit #6: Going into Workaholic Mode

"Gonna put the world away for a minute, pretend I don't live in it" – Zac Brown Band

We've talked about how to stay on top of your goals and how to manage them to make them realities. Now let's talk about what it's like to work too hard towards those goals, or in general.

Work too hard? Did she just tell me not to put in the absolute most I can towards my goals? Doesn't that go against everything she just said?

Not quite my friend. I'm talking about exploring the difference between putting in hard work and overworking yourself.

I am a full-blown workaholic.

I plan my days out before they begin so I can maximize my time and get done what I need to get done. It helps to make me a very productive person and it calms my anxiety to know what I have to get done in a day. The downside is when I have a second to sit down and do something that isn't working towards my physical health, my job, or building my personal brand as a trainer, I get a little confused. It feels wrong. Why am I just sitting here in bed? Isn't there something I'm supposed to be doing? I could be using this time to work towards XYZ instead of watching Netflix.

Like I mentioned earlier, I have a routine for myself to make sure I work towards my goals and stay on track with my priorities every day. Some days my to-do list is longer than others. On the short days, I often find myself feeling guilty about using my time to do anything other than something that could be making me money or putting me in better shape, etc. I have this need to always be doing something productive or to always be working.

This is not healthy behavior. There is a fine line between getting what you need to get done and stressing yourself out so you never have a moment to yourself.

Growing up, I was always pushed to be a step ahead of everyone else. My dad grew up an immigrant with foreign parents and didn't have much guidance in his education or life at all, really. When he became a dad, he pushed me and my brother to be the best we could be in all aspects because that was something he wishes he had as a child.

On the other hand, my mom was very disciplined her whole life. She was an excellent student and every mom's dream child. Seriously, she dusted her room every single Saturday … willingly. I think I can count on my hands how many times I've dusted my room on a Saturday. She encouraged us to carry the same work ethic she has with us in our school work, sports, jobs, etc.

I am fortunate to have parents who cared about my success and pushed me to do well. I spent my elementary years filling out summer workbooks to exercise my brain and participating in our local library's summer reading challenge. My brother and I grew up playing with things like Brain Quest and Leapfrog. I constantly read books to him when I was old enough to read and he was young enough to let me.

Growing up, I feared to disappoint my parents and yearned for the praise they gave me when I went above and beyond everyone else. I was always in the accelerated math classes, I was in the gifted and talented program in elementary school, I was placed in the highest reading groups ever since I learned how to read. In high school I was in a specialized learning program because why just attend high school like a normal kid when you can join a specialized learning program, I guess.

I felt like I always needed to be the best. As I grew older, it became less about what my parents thought of me and more what I thought of me. It made me feel good internally knowing I was in the highest-level classes in high school or that I was exempt from taking classes in college because of AP scores.

Now that I'm at the tail-end of my college career, the majority of my everyday activities revolve around how much I'll stand out on your resume. I worked not one but two internships in my sophomore year of college because I wanted to stand out at the career fair in the fall. I push myself to do better than my friends on exams so my GPA will stand out on my resume. I made a dang website to kickstart my personal training business and to prove my marketing skills on my resume. The list continues.

There's nothing wrong with wanting to stand out and be a step ahead of everyone else. Standing out is what gets you noticed by employers or by affiliate programs or whatever it is you're in search of. However, when you're five steps ahead of everyone else that's when it's time to close the books, clock out, and live a little!

Are you the type of person who spends dawn to dusk studying away in the library? Or the girl who's working three jobs to pay her rent? Or someone who's part of five different clubs that all meet on different nights of the week just so you can have leadership experience on your resume? If you are, let me ask you a few things:

Do you think your work ethic is healthy?

Does the amount of time you spend working affect your social or family relationships?

How ahead are you than the rest of your peers?

Some people need to study for long periods before their brain comprehends things. Some people come from financial situations where they need to work to make ends meet or repay loans. Hard work is what makes us reach our goals and live our dreams. But is the amount that you're working taking away joy from your life? Is it giving you a constant feeling of anxiety?

A strong work ethic is one of the most rewarding characteristics to have. That work ethic comes with knowing when to stop and smell the roses in your life. Sometimes the time we spend working can affect the relationships we have in our lives. During my first two summers after college I barely saw anyone the entire three months because I was working three jobs. I didn't have to work three jobs but I love getting paid and the opportunities presented themselves. I put myself through the stress because I hated having too much time to spare and I wanted to make money, then when my friends wanted to hang out I was too busy.

I'm not saying you need to relax completely. I am definitely an advocate for hard work. There's a balance we can meet to ensure we're putting in our work but also devoting some time to do the things we enjoy in life, whatever that might be for you.

Improvement #6: Spend One Hour Every Day Doing Something You Enjoy Doing

Life is a freaking marathon.

Every day there are things that need to be done – shifts that need to be worked, homework that needs to be done, club meetings that need to be attended, groceries that need to be bought, etc. For a workaholic, those busy days are even busier because that need and love for working prolong your time spent working, leaving less time in the day for yourself.

As I said, I struggle with overworking. It not only affects my social relationships sometimes but it puts a lot more stress on me than is warranted. For a long time, I felt like a minute I spent relaxing was a minute wasted that I could've been doing something productive.

And then it hit me.

Taking care of myself is being productive too.

It's not productive in the sense that it's getting my homework out of the way or making me money, it's productive in the sense that I am improving my mental health and my happiness.

I started to take one hour a day to do something that isn't working towards any goals, it's just something that I enjoy. To be clear, this is separate from my workouts. Although my workouts are my time to be alone and blow some steam, they're a part of my routine and work towards my health-oriented goals.

Everyone's idea of leisure activities is different. For you, spending an hour of doing something you enjoy might include getting a workout in or yoga in. For me, I choose to spend this hour differently every day based on my mood. Sometimes this means getting up an hour earlier so I can have breakfast alone and sit on my phone just scrolling. Yesterday, I spent an hour after work painting a picture of a butterfly for no other reason than I enjoy painting and thought it would look cool on my wall at my apartment.

The point is, we should all have an hour every day to ourselves.

If you're thinking right now, this woman's crazy, doesn't she know what it's like to be in college? My life is a total marathon. I have class, then work, then the gym, then a chapter meeting and then I have to study. I don't have an hour to myself, lady, then that right there is a problem within itself.

If you can't find an hour to give to yourself in the day then you need to take a step back and ask yourself why you're doing everything you're doing and make some adjustments.

There's no wrong or right time to spend time with yourself. This hour can be the first hour you get up or the last hour you're awake. It could be smack in the middle of the day when you're eating lunch, I don't care! All that is important is that you take time each day to do something for yourself.

If I could fit in two jobs (one being a 9-5), a workout, and time in the library all in one day and still find time for myself, so can you.

I stress the importance of taking time to ourselves because we only have one shot on this earth. Yep, you only get one go at life. If you spend your whole life working towards a goal, what will you have to look back on once you've reached it?

I preach about goals every day on Instagram. I just preached to you for two whole chapters on goals. When I reach mine, I want to look back and know that I was happy in the time I spent working towards it. If you're miserable working towards something, ask yourself, is this really what I want? Or, is there anything I can be doing to make myself a little happier right now?

Every semester I have the goal of achieving a 4.0 GPA. Mind you, I still stand firmly in my opinion that homework is unenjoyable and studying is equally as painful as stabbing pens in my eyes. Despite how unenjoyable it is, I work every day towards this goal because I know the GPA will make me stand out.

The old me would stay in the library until I was certain I knew everything for my exam on my first night of studying, and my brain would feel like its bleeding by the night's end.

Present me makes a study to-do list and closes the books when that list is over. Then I go home, put on a face mask, and listen to some music or read depending on the day. My time to myself, whenever it is, is my time to recharge and unwind so my brain is ready for a new day tomorrow.

Still not convinced? Still not sure how you can fit this into your schedule? My advice to you is to make some lists. Every morning when I journal I make a checklist of the things I need to get done and sometimes I include a time-line if it's applicable. This allows me to see where I have room to take time for myself.

Throughout everything we do and everything we work towards, it's important not to lose ourselves. Mental health is just as important as physical health and part of making sure we're okay is making sure we have time to give back to ourselves.

Habit #7: Eating Like Crap

"Every time you eat or drink, you are either feeding disease or fighting it" – Heather Morgan

Taking care of yourself can be done in so many ways. One of them is taking time to do things you enjoy, as we just talked about. Another is making sure you're nourishing your body.

I'm sure at some point you've heard or read someone preaching about how "your body is a temple" and rolled your eyes. Quite frankly, the phrase makes me roll my eyes too but there's truth behind what they're saying.

The cool thing about bodies is that everything, literally everything, we do in a day affects our bodies, internally and externally. The way we feed our bodies is especially important because it affects not only our physique but our brains as well.

Remember my Dorito/Oreo/Everything-Bad-For-You phase I talked about earlier? Well, I'm going to resurface the shameful topic. If you're feeling hungry, I would grab a healthy snack before we jump into all this food talk.

I was pretty thin as a child. I'm talking pre-pubescent years here. I had rock-solid abs until I was about 13 years old just by genetic nature and playing sports as a child. My mom always fed us healthy dinners, composed of meat and veggies, and we seldom had the sugary and fun cereals in my house. Every once in a while, she would buy Captain Crunch or Reese's Puffs, and my brother and I would go absolutely bananas and finish the box in two days. Other than that, it was pretty much Special K or Honey Bunches of Oats for breakfast every morning. Maybe the occasional Eggo.

One thing we were always loaded with: snacks.

I'm not talking Ring Dings and Cosmic Brownies, my mom knew better than that, but we were always stacked with Lays, Chips Ahoy, and my personal favorite: microwave popcorn.

Would you believe me if I told you that every day in seventh grade I came home and made myself a personal bag of microwavable kettle corn? It's true, I really did. In my house, we have a drawer in the kitchen just for snacks. We also had a separate cabinet to store the unopened ones. I've lost track of the number of times my brother and I got scolded for having too many snacks open in the drawer. Most of the time the dang thing could barely shut without something getting crinkled.

I had some sort of a concept of what eating healthy was like. Apples were good, Twinkies were bad - you know, the basics. As a child, I was never really concerned. I was eating all the Cheetos I wanted and I looked pretty dang good for a 12-year-old.

I wish someone had taught me the importance of proper nutrition when I was younger because my snacking and eating habits stayed with me as I grew older. Sure, in health we learned about the food pyramid and all that but no one ever taught me about eating foods with simple ingredients and how the amount of food you consume calorie-wise can have an effect on your body.

Instead, all I learned was that sweets are on the top of the food pyramid and high-fructose corn syrup is not good for you. Thanks, PE department.

You know what else they never bothered to teach us? The foods we ate affect our brains and moods.

Our bodies produce serotonin which regulates things like sleep and mood for us. Most of this serotonin is controlled by the bacteria in our intestines. If you don't believe me, read this quote from the professionals at Harvard Medical:

"Since about 95% of your serotonin is produced in your gastrointestinal tract, and your gastrointestinal tract is lined with a hundred million nerve cells, or neurons, it makes sense that the inner workings of your digestive system don't just help you digest food, but also guide your emotions" (Eva Selhub MD).

Put simply, the things we eat control what our body produces and what our body produces controls things like our mood.

Whole foods that are full of vitamins and minerals literally help to fuel our brain while processed foods do quite the opposite.

Would eating a nutritious diet of whole foods have cured my depression in high school? Not all together, but it would've been a step in the right direction. It also would've kept my skin a little clearer, which is a bonus. I don't know about you but when I eat too much sugar, all of a sudden, my t-zone looks like a volcano erupted right there in between my eyebrows. I dislike looking like that.

Eating healthy goes way beyond your physical appearance. You might have the fastest metabolism known to mankind but just because you can eat Frito's and still have rock solid abs doesn't mean you're immune to the harmful effects of junk food. Eating better is scientifically proven to make you feel better. As a bonus, you're helping to promote your overall longevity.

My brother has a much faster metabolism than I do. Puberty didn't quite hit us the same. When I have one single Oreo, my stomach instantly bloats three inches. Brendan, on the other hand, can eat five Elios' pizzas in a day and still have a body fat percentage of, like, nine. It's not fair, but it is life.

After years of my nagging and not so subtle encouragement, he's finally beginning to understand why it's important for him to care of his diet as well. Sure, he's not gaining weight from the junk food he eats, but it's elevating his cholesterol and clogging his arteries with fatty acids. Think of all that yellowy, clumpy fat that circulates through your bloodstream and throughout your stomach after you eat a fried chicken sandwich from Wendy's. Gross, right?

There are so many other harmful effects that eating a poor diet can have on your body and I'm sure you've heard of them at some point in your life. As we grow older and older, the risk of medical emergencies like heart attacks become and a more likely possibility. Have you ever heard the phrase, "you can't work off a bad diet"? This is what that phrase means.

Have I convinced you to drop the Flaming Hot Cheeto's yet?

If I haven't, let's shift our focus to your body goals. Eating like crap is definitely taking a step backward in achieving your dream bod. Diet and exercise work hand and hand. You can work out all you want but if your diet is pretty much garbage, change will happen but not in the direction you want it to be in.

Maybe you're happy with where your body is at. If you are, I'm happy for you! But I also encourage you to think deeper about our talk on longevity.

Maybe you want to lose body fat. Cutting out the high-calorie snacks and meals is important for you then.

Maybe you want to build muscle. Getting enough protein every day is important for you then.

Whatever your personal goals are, it's important to nourish your body properly and consistently to get you there. This doesn't mean you have to close the door to ice cream forever – I continue to have my meetups with my pals Ben and Jerry and will never abandon them, but I do so in moderation. I'm not snacking on ice cream four nights a week but if my friends want to go out to Jersey Freeze, I'm all in!

Eating a healthy diet is not the easiest thing to adapt to while at college, especially if you eat at a dining hall. I get asked all the time how I manage to eat at my school's café's and dining halls and maintain my diet.

Is it easy? No, not at first.

Is it possible? Most definitely.

It's much easier to order takeout when you're studying for hours in the library. It's much more convenient to order breakfast ahead on the Starbucks app than get up a few minutes earlier and cook for yourself before class. It's cheaper to buy a bag of chips in the vending machine versus a protein bar. I get it. But remember our list of priorities? Where do your health and longevity fall on your list?

I'll tell you this much, none of your other priorities matter if you're not alive to focus on them.

Eating a healthy diet while living at school is completely achievable. It might take a while to adapt to the change and to figure out what choices to make, but it is achievable nonetheless. How do I know? I do so every day.

The following improvement is one of the steps that help making a healthy diet while at school attainable.

Improvement #7: Base Your Diet Around Clean Foods

I noticed a significant change in my mood and my skin when I cracked down on what I was eating. Those greasy zones on my face are clear 95% of the time now. I don't feel tired or sluggish after I eat, I feel energized and ready to move.

The easiest way to get yourself to stop eating junk food is to stop buying it. Junk food is cheaper, I know. As college kids, we're always trying to find the cheaper options to save a few bucks. This food is cheaper for a reason, though. Let me give you a quick economics lesson.

Goods and services are priced so the business makes a profit. The cheaper it is to make something, the cheaper that product can afford to be sold.

Why can Wendy's afford to have a four for four promotion? Because it costs pebbles to make their food. How does it make you feel knowing you're eating something that costs nothing to make? Does it feel satisfying to fill your body with stuff that is so cheap that it can be sold at one dollar? That's what I thought.

We're in college, we can't afford to be shopping at Whole Foods every week, I get it! Honestly, I've never been inside of a Whole Foods in my life. A few things that have helped me spend less along the way: coupons, sales, and buying less overall. Couponing is tedious. I bet when I said couponing you immediately thought of a 70-year-old Grandma snipping from grocery store flyers at her kitchen table. Imagine if you saved even just five dollars every time you shopped? Those five dollars are going to add up every week!

Also, screw Whole Foods.

Sorry, I said it. I just offended a bunch of Californians who only shop at organic grocery stores and pay double the amount for the same things you can find in Trader Joe's. Whole Foods is nice and all and if I had the money I would shop there too but I'm a college student and healthy options exist in other places besides Whole Foods.

Y'all, Trader Joe's is the holy land. I'm serious.

No really, their produce is a little on the expensive side but you can find some seriously good deals there! My personal favorite is the unsweetened acai packets that go for four dollars a bag. That's a freaking steal and they're unsweetened. I'm a sucker for cutting out sugar when I can. Oh, I also love their teeny tiny avocados. I mean, they're cute and fairly priced! Don't even get me started on the shredded hash browns …

Okay, I'm going to get back to my point before I go devote a good three pages to how much I love Trader Joe's.

Centering your diet around clean and simple foods helps eliminate all the unnecessary crap that can be harmful to your body and your mood, as we talked about earlier. This winter I went through my bulking phase and was eating the most calories I have in my life, yet my body fat actually dropped because I had modified by diet to be simpler and cleaner than it was previously.

My dinners typically consist of chicken, a vegetable, and a carb such as brown rice or potatoes (I am the world's largest advocate for potatoes – shredded potatoes, mashed potatoes, roasted potatoes, they're all special). I also like to choose unsweetened foods when I can such as unsweetened almond milk or sugar-free ketchup. At first it was a little shocking but once you get used to it, the sugar-filled options make your teeth want to fall off right on the spot. It's a great way to cut the crap and unnecessary calories from your diet.

I realize changing the way you eat is a big request to ask of you. I don't expect anyone to change their diet and their pallet overnight. You can start small and progress forward.

Start by replacing one food that you regularly eat with a healthier option. For example, start replacing your morning Eggo's with Kodiak Cakes or whole wheat waffles. Maybe you want to replace your afternoon bag of chips with an apple. Or how about replacing cream cheese on your bagel for avocado? Whatever it is, start with one replacement and then work your way to the next.

Once you stop buying and start replacing, a healthy diet becomes so much more attainable. After all, if it's not in your house it won't be there to tempt you. After a while, you'll begin to enjoy and look forward to your healthy replacements. I know this is going to sound freakish but I love caramel rice cakes. Holy crap I love them so much. I look forward to getting to eat them. It makes me happier knowing that I look forward to these choices instead of feeling sad that I'm not eating cookies.

Good riddance, Doritos!

One of my biggest inspirations along the way was Jill Christine Fit's Instagram. I don't know her actual name, all I know is her username so I'm going to assume her first name is Jill.

Anyway, I was watching her responses to a Q and A one day and someone had asked her how she "beats her cravings". She responded by saying that she craves the healthy foods she eats. What she eats every day is her diet but it's not a diet. She lives her life without restrictions because she genuinely enjoys what she eats every day and looks forward to eating it.

I read that and thought dang, that is so achievable.

Eating healthy is not black and white, there are so many foods you can combine and recipes you can try to make things interesting for you – my favorite meal right now is an acai bowl. I use acai and vanilla whey protein for the base. I top it off with raspberries, granola, chia seeds, and almond butter. It's half the calories of a bowl from Playa Bowls and still so satisfying! I get eager every day around lunchtime.

The point is, you can fit in clean and simple foods into your life without depriving yourself. When people ask me what I'm eating, I like to be able to tell them exactly what is on my plate, I'm eating chicken, brown rice, and sweet potato fries with cinnamon that I air-fried myself!

Start slow, and work new things into your diet.

Do it for your mood. Do it to beat the gas you get after dinner (gross I know, but I'm sure you've gone through it). Do it for the acne you've been trying to clear up. Do it to build more muscle and become a strong woman, literally and mentally. Do it so you live to see one hundred years.

CH. 8

Habit #8: Letting Other People Determine My Happiness

"You must not let anyone define your limits because of where you come from. Your only limit is your soul" – Gustaeu, Ratatouille

I just had a meltdown.

I just had my first meltdown in almost a month, and that meltdown was the first I'd had in the month-span before that.

The cause behind today's meltdown was a fight with my father. I love my dad with my whole, entire heart, and most of the time he is such an awesome, cool, fun dad. But like most families, mine has its downsides. Let me tell you a quick version of our story.

My parents had an unusual divorce. Normally when someone describes their divorce they describe it as a big ugly mess or months of household warfare leading up to the final bomb explosion. My parents' divorce was somewhat … civil. The split happened when I was 13, the divorce when I was 17.

The story behind why my parents are no longer married is not the point here nor is it my story to tell but its' important to point out because it makes sense then why I got to see my dad quite regularly as a kid. I lived with my mom while he lived in a new house alone. Since my parents get along, he visited quite frequently throughout the week which was always such a nice surprise for me.

At the end of my senior year of high school, things started to change. One day in June, my dad had suggested we go work out together at the YMCA. I was thrilled because I had no concept of how to go about weight lifting and going with my dad would prevent me from walking around the gym like a lost child.

That was the day he taught me what 21's are. If you're unfamiliar, 21's are a bicep curl variation that consists of 21 reps in one set and is honestly cruel to your arms. My little arms were dead meat that day. When the workout was over, we got in his car so he could take me back home.

"So, I have to tell you something," He said.

Uh oh.

Most of the time I've been approached with that opening, the following statement was something that is guaranteed to ruin my mood. I stayed silent. "I decided to have Karen and her kids move in so I could start my next chapter with her."

My heart stopped right there in that car. Karen (Karen is not her real name, I decided to leave that out and Karen was the first thing that popped into my brain), was the mother of my adorable baby half-sister, Jenna. To my knowledge, they weren't even *dating* let alone ready to move in together. So yeah, I was pretty shocked.

Every negative emotion I could've possibly felt rushed into my body. I was angry that he buttered me up with a workout before telling me this. I was hurt that he lied about his relationship with this woman. I felt betrayed that other kids would be living with my dad when I didn't even live with him and I'm his first-born child. I felt like these people were stealing my dad from me. The thought of him being a father-figure to anyone else made me want to puke.

I said absolutely nothing. Radio silence.

When we got to my house I ran up to my room, buried my face into my pillows, and cried my heart out. I called my friends and asked them if I could come over so I could be as far away as possible from my dad.

That was the first time I felt like I had lost my father.

I cried for the majority of that entire night. I asked God why he had put me through this. I hadn't asked for this, I was a good kid – I didn't smoke weed, I barely ever drank, I didn't lie, steal, or cheat, I was a straight-A student … why was this happening to me?

I had a close friend at that time who had a picture-perfect family. His family enjoyed spending time with each other, his parents went on dates even after their kids were all grown, and he had such a close relationship with all of them. They looked out for each other. They got along.

The more time we spent together or I spent around them, the deeper I fell into a hole of self-pity. I looked at his family and constantly compared it to mine. I was green with jealousy, wishing I could trade places with him.

I looked at his family and judged mine based on his.

Time healed the hurt I was feeling that day and life moved on. After I moved away to school, gym sessions with dad turned into dinners with dad somewhere near school. I pushed aside my responsibilities to make time for him because I loved being able to see him and because I got to eat real food that wasn't manufactured by Sodexo.

When my brother was old enough, he followed my footsteps to Rutgers and began to join in on our weekly dinners. One night in October, Dad asked us if we were available to get dinner. I said yes, as always, and began daydreaming about Chipotle and Honeygrow as I sat on the Business School mezzanine.

And then he told me he was bringing Jenna.

I love Jenna but for a long time, it was really hard for me to be around her. She is so much younger than me and whenever we were together, she was the center of my dad's attention. I felt like I didn't matter to him when she was there because she was his new baby girl and I was an old college kid.

News flash, college kids still need their dad's too.

I answered back, voicing my hesitations about her joining us. This was my time with my dad and I selfishly wanted it to myself. I wanted my one hour a week where my dad was just my dad again.

He blew up on me.

Do you know what it's like to have a parent from a Chinese upbringing, who was also very high up in the law enforcement field, blow up on you? The two backgrounds are a very powerful and frightening combination. It's enough to make you want to crawl back inside the womb and pretend you were never born at all. I'm not kidding here.

He canceled our plans for the night and quite frankly canceled me from his life as well. He told me how much of a disappointment I was to him – those words will always hurt me. I don't remember the exact words that were exchanged in the rest of the conversation but I do remember the tears I cried. No, more like the tears I screamed and spilled out of my eyes like that scene in Frozen II when (spoiler alert) the dam broke.

We didn't speak for over a month after that. During that time was when I found out my mom had cancer and he still didn't speak or reach out to me.

One night shortly after this blow-up, I went to Applebee's with my friends and then-boyfriend. My stomach was bothering me the whole time we were there and I'm honestly still surprised I didn't end up throwing up in the backseat of the car. When we got back to my house, my boyfriend came in to make sure I was okay. We got to my room, sat down on my bed, and I broke down crying.

I sobbed my freaking eyes out and just curled up into a ball in his arms.

Words began to flood out of my mouth about how upset I was with my dad and how I wished that I could just have a normal family. I kept apologizing for crying as he comforted me. I had no idea why in that sudden moment I had broken down. The only feasible answer I could come up with is that I was letting my dad and the circumstances of my family control my happiness.

I thought about my friends' family in high school. It occurred to me at that moment that I had done the same thing then.

For years, I got myself worked up over the actions of my family remembers. I longed for the type of families I saw around me which made me resent my family's situation even more. I looked at other people's happy families and it made mine seem so broken. I let this pain fester up inside of me and control how I lived every day.

I let it send me into a deep depression when I was 18 because I wanted things to be different.

Improvement #8: Take What You're Unhappy with and Use it as Your Motivation and Inspiration

How many times have you gone on Instagram and thought badly about your body after seeing a picture of a model or even the pretty girl from your calc class?

How many times have you stalked through fitness accounts and thought "I'm not fit enough" or "I'm not strong enough"?

How many times has the kid next to you get a better grade than you on an exam and you think, "I'm not smart enough"?

How many times have you been envious of a friend who landed an internship or a job that you wanted and you haven't secured one yet?

If you've done any of the above, you've let someone control your happiness and opinion about yourself or life.

Other people's successes and failures do not define that of yours.

My parents screwed up. Most parents do in some way. For years, I kicked myself and asked God why this was happening to me. I compared my family to my friends' families and cried about how I wish I could trade places with them.

What happened between my parents does not define me. That is something that took me years and years to realize.

It is hard sometimes when they really hurt me and there are times where my tears are warranted. But after I let it out, I dry them up and move on, knowing that one day I will have my own family and I'll get to decide how our household is.

Instead of wallowing about the unfortunate situation of my family, I now look at it and realize there is hope for my future. First of all, I'm lucky to even have two parents who are alive. Second, their mistakes will guide me in determining, and eventually creating, the type of household and family that I want in my future. Every day is one step closer to having a household that I am in control of. I turned my tears into hope. Seeing the bright in the situation feels a lot better than spending hours crying silently into my pillow.

The same idea can be applied to most aspects of our lives. Just because your friend gets a full-time job offer before you, doesn't mean that you failed at getting a job. Who cares if she got one first? Instead of being bitter, congratulate her and work towards your vision of landing a full-time job.

Do most of your friends have boyfriends yet you're going on 22 and still single? That's great for them that they've found love. Just because you haven't found the right person yet doesn't mean you've failed and will die alone. Dying along is a common assumption made by the single population.

Did your classmate post about her 4.0 GPA this semester while you finished with a 3.5? That doesn't mean you're not a great student. That doesn't mean you failed the semester. If you tried your hardest, you should be proud of the grades you received. Be happy for her and aspire to achieve a 4.0 next semester.

There is always someone who will be blonder than you, skinnier than you, stronger than you, smarter than you, more artistic than you, the list goes on. You're that person for someone else. We are all born different and good at different things.

My roommate Elaina is by far funnier than me. She's one of the funniest people I've ever met in my life, seriously her personality belongs on a morning talk show or something. While she beats me in the comedy department, I can lift heavier weights than her.

The thing about me and Elaina is we don't find each other's strengths to be our weaknesses. Elaina constantly praises me for the time I spend in the gym when she could easily turn the inspiration she gets from me into jealously.

On my side, I always give her positive feedback on the funny videos she posts on social media because they genuinely crack me up. Plus, I know the positive comments will make her smile. I could sit in my room and be jealous that she's getting thousands of TikTok views a day and practically going viral. Instead, I look at her internet success as inspiration to keep pursuing my own accounts and inspiring my own following. Her success does not determine my failure.

Jealousy is one of the most disgusting feelings to possess. And where does that feeling really get us besides deep into a bad attitude?

I stopped looking at other people's successes as my failures and looked at them as inspiration to set goals for myself. I stopped letting the failures of my family and friends affect my life and motivation. I am in complete control of every emotion I feel and how long it lasts.

Today when my dad and I got into another fight. I came home and cried for a few minutes and then I picked myself up out of my puddle of tears and created something good from it.

I grabbed my journal and wrote down 5 things I want in a family when I grow up. It doesn't change what's happening to me right now, but it gives me hope for the future and sets my expectations clear. It reminds me that I can be in control of my emotions. I'm done wishing my family circumstances were different. I'm done feeling jealous of other people's situations. I am in control of my own happiness.

In this day and age, we compare ourselves to the people around us more than we recognize. It's hard as a young woman to stop comparing myself to others. Social media makes it even harder. There are two ways you can look at a social media post. You can look at it and feel like a failure or you can look at it and feel inspired. It's up to you how you want to feel at the end of the day. Living your life as a comparison to others brings us back to habit number 1 that we're trying to bust: improving yourself for someone else.

Your happiness is determined by what you make of every situation.

Some things will happen to us that we can't explain but that doesn't have to define how well our lives are going. My family is a little broken, most peoples are, but at the end of the day, I still have two parents and two siblings who wake up each morning breathing, and one day I will have one of my own.

Habit #9: Faking It

"I have to realize that every time I begin to lose confidence, it's NOT because I am insecure but because I simply FEEL insecure. And there's a difference" – Jordan Lee Dooley

My first big-girl interview was for a company called Savvy Marketers. I had applied for an intern position online as a sophomore, not expecting much because I was so young. When I got the call they wanted me to come in for an interview, I was ecstatic!

When the interview day came, I straightened my hair, perfected my makeup with a nice simple look, and carefully put on my business suit. And then… I got into my mom's car so she could drive me.

I felt like such a fraud, such a baby. Here I was in my professional suit but my mommy still had to drive me and wait for me in the car.

The reason why my mom was taking me was that, like many college students, I didn't have my car at school at the time. Up until a month later, I had shared a car with my little brother who was a senior in high school. He used the car to drive to school every day.

Looking back on it, it's completely reasonable why my mom had to drive me and I mean, what else was I supposed to do? But at the moment, I felt like such a phony. I felt like I was pretending to be this big girl who was kickstarting her career but I couldn't even drive myself to my own dang interview.

I always felt like a phony going on interviews. I would hype up my work experiences to make myself seem more experienced than I really felt like I was, in hopes of impressing the interviewer. I looked at other candidate's job experiences and wondered how I would ever compare. I'm just a kid.

One of my internships was with Sky Blue FC, a professional soccer team, the summer after my sophomore year. It involved a ton of manual labour, all of which was to make sure the games ran smoothly and gave the fans the optimal event experience. It wasn't your typical 9-5 office internship but I got to come face to face with freaking Olympians and it was pretty dang cool.

When interviewers would ask me about my experience with Sky Blue I would say something along the lines of, "It taught me a lot about working with different types of people and the importance of cooperating in teams to complete tasks". Very sophisticated response, I know. I left out the part where I was carrying field boards three times my size across a professional soccer field or getting soaked from head-to-toe by sprinklers to protect fans from getting wet. I hoped, I prayed, they wouldn't see through my response.

I thought, why on earth would these interviewers care at all about my summer work?
I felt like my internship didn't compare to what other people were doing. Sure, I was an "intern" but I wanted to be sitting at an air-conditioned desk with a fancy laptop, not sweating through my shirt on a soccer field. I didn't feel like a real intern at all.

I made myself believe I wasn't a real intern. Consequently, when it came time for interviews, I made myself believe I was faking it when it came to having experience.

I was beyond nervous when I was assigned my first ever client as a personal trainer. Sure, I had passed my exam and had plenty of experience in the gym but now another person's physical health was my responsibility! I felt so inexperienced at personal training during the beginning because, well, I was.

The night before my first workout with my first client, I spent hours going over what type of workout I would give her. I thought of every possibility of things that could go wrong. What if I made it too hard for her? What if I made it too easy? What if my boss saw me working and thought I wasn't doing a good enough job? What if she hates me? Am I supposed to bark at her like a coach? Is she going to think I'm mean if I correct her form?

I felt like a fraud for the entire session. I felt like I was faking being a personal trainer. Instead of realizing that everyone has to start at the beginning, I felt like I was playing pretend. I didn't let myself believe that I really was a personal trainer. For a while, each time I put on my shirt that read "trainer" in bright red letters on the back, I felt so silly. I braced myself to walk into the College Ave Gym and pretend to be this all-knowing personal trainer.

A few months later while I was waiting for a client to arrive, I noticed a student running very dangerously on the treadmill. He was holding onto the handles at a very high speed and leaning back as he ran. If he lost his grip, he would've been eaten alive by the treadmill.

Now, I don't like to judge what people are doing in the gym because I know everyone is at different stages of their fitness journey. However, it concerns me when I see someone doing something that could physically put them in danger. The way this student was running could not only cause serious damage to his shins but he could get really hurt if his hands happened to slip.

I had no idea what to do.

My boss had told us that if we're wearing our trainer shirt and we ask the person first if they want to receive a helpful tip from us, we are allowed to step in on dangerous situations that we come across (it's important to always ask someone in the gym if they want your help first because people, ahem like me, can get really offended if you just step in and offer your unwanted opinion). The fitness assistants had noticed this guy too and wondered what to do. We all looked at each other with blank stares.

"Well, you're a trainer, can't you say something?" They asked.

I was so morally conflicted. A part of me knew that I could step in, yet I hesitated. Who says this man wants my opinion? What if I embarrass him? What if he never comes back to the gym after this? Who am I to tell him he's doing something wrong?

Hesitantly, I stepped into the office and asked my boss what to do. She had also noticed the dangerous situation and reassured me that I could step in and ask him if he wanted my opinion. Despite her affirmation, I remained hesitant.

I ended up staying in my spot against the back wall of the gym, keeping my mouth close, and my nose in my own business. In hindsight, this was morally wrong of me. The feeling that I had about "faking it" when it came to my position is what held me back. If I hadn't been so filled with self-doubt, I would've stepped in. Instead, I had myself convinced that I was too new and too inexperienced to do anything.

In both of these situations, I felt like I was pretending to be someone instead of recognizing that I actually was that someone all along.

My years spent in college so far have been a period of kickstarting things. With every day and every class, I take, I'm learning more about what I like and don't like and what inspires me.
I've been on countless interviews, I've taken exams to get certifications, I've joined different clubs and tried new jobs, the whole nine yards. But because of how young I am and because I'm still in college, everything I do seems like I'm doing the junior version. In other words, I don't feel like "the real deal".

This mindset made me go to work and feel like I was the "intern" instead of a real employee. I would go on interviews and think, I'm just a college student, I don't have any real experience under my belt. I spent zero time embracing who I was and the experience I've gained and spent all of my time doubting myself.

Then I started listening to the She podcast by Jordan Lee Dooley.

I was never a podcast type of gal, I prefer to listen to music. Will you keep a secret? I accidentally stopped listening to Call Her Daddy. Don't tell the other college girls, they'll gasp. The She podcast is different. It's captivating and enlightening and welcoming.

In one episode. Jordan talked about a subject that really hit home for me, even though she used it in a context beyond a college student's experience. She talks about imposter syndrome. Imposter syndrome is this term Jordan uses for when the pressure to prove yourself begins to take over. She talks about her first sales on Etsy and how she didn't believe herself to really be an entrepreneur, it was just something fun she was doing because she liked it. When she said this I thought, *but Jordan, if you're selling your own goods, doesn't that make you an entrepreneur?* Sometimes we think too little of ourselves and feel too much pressure to realize who we actually are.

When I heard Jordan talk about imposter syndrome for the first time I clicked pause immediately.

The realization hit me like a ton of bricks.

All this time I felt like I was pretending to be someone or something instead of owning the fact that I was actually doing the damn thing.

Improvement #9: Owning Who I Am

All this time, it became natural for me to slip into this belief that I'm not important enough because I'm just a college kid. I'm only 21 years old and have never had a full-time job before unlike the people I work alongside.

Are you selling your products that you've made? You are an entrepreneur.

Did you land a new internship in field sales for the summer? You are a marketer.

Did you recently get elected as the president of your club? You are a leader.

One of my interviews last fall was with Toyota. When the interviewers asked me to elaborate on my internship experience, I used my typical response to talk about Sky Blue. Something different happened next. This time, instead of a nod some jotting down of words, I got a pretty enlightening response.

One of the two interviewers told me he worked for a professional lacrosse team on the side and that seeing that I've had experience with event productions for a professional sports team showed a lot about my work ethic to him and what I've gone through. He knew because he's been through it all.

Boom. It hit me.

All this time I was hiding aspects of my job experience because I felt like if I skirted around them, it would make me appear to be a better worker. If I had been completely transparent with my experience, the interviewers would've seen how hard of a worker I am and how driven my work ethic is.

I am a hard worker. I am a good marketer. This whole time I was faking it through interviews, feeling as if I was pretending to be someone that I actually am.

When it comes to personal training, it took me a long time to stop faking it and just be it. It sounds simple. It sounds silly. I have my certification so why did I feel so hesitant about stepping in when I noticed a dangerous situation occurring in the gym?

Because I was faking who I was instead of just embracing and acting like who I am.

Does that make sense? Do I sound silly saying this?

If I had pushed away my insecurities about being young and having only a little experience, I would've been able to step in and help the patron without any qualms. Of course, I was inexperienced at first, everyone has to have their first client. That doesn't mean I'm not a personal trainer, I have the certificate to prove it.

Once I allowed myself to accept my role for what it was, I stopped getting nervous about writing workouts. I stopped getting nervous about what my clients would think of me. I started owning who I was and using the knowledge I had rightfully acquired to be the best I could be at my job.

Who cares if my boss was watching form her office? I am a certified personal trainer and I know what I am doing in the gym.

There's no doubt that when you're in college, you're not going to be as experienced in anything really as people who have already graduated. That's what college is for. It's during this time that we get out first roles in big companies or our first leadership roles, etc.

Last year I worked for an insurance company as an intern. Was my title role just an "intern"? Yes. But was I still an employee? Yes. My role in the company may have been lower on the office hierarchy scale compared to the other insurance agents and full-time employees, but I was still rightfully an employee. I came in with assigned tasks to complete every day. During my time in the office, I felt so silly coming in as a 19-year-old when everyone else old enough to have children or be engaged. I realize now that I was just as much a part of the business as they were, even though I was a decade younger than everyone.

Everyone always refers to college as the "fake real world". Have you noticed that? I remember my high school economics teacher told us once to soak up every minute of college because after that I was doomed to enter the "real world".

The phrase holds a little bit of truth in it. I certainly haven't started owning up to all my adult responsibilities yet. On the flip side, I think this term can be confusing and is used way too often that it puts the false concept in our brains. Some of us start jobs, some of us pay our utilities and rent, some of us are working co-ops all day and then take classes all night long!
The "fake real world" assumes just that. It assumes that what you're doing isn't real.

Of course, it's real!

Maybe you're not working a 9-5 corporate job yet, that doesn't mean you're not still valuable to the company you're interning for. Maybe you're in your first month at a new job as a Zumba instructor at the rec center. Yes, you're new to it, but that doesn't make you any less of an instructor. Use all the Zumba knowledge you have and lead that class with confidence.

While we're talking about phrases I hate, I'm not a fan of the term "fake it until you make it" either. I'm even less of a fan of the fact my seventh grade English teacher spent the whole year imprinting this phrase into my mouldable, young brain.

If you show up and do the work, that is who you are. Unless we're talking about using your older sister's ID at the bar, you're not faking anything.

Stop spending your college years pretending to be someone. Stop putting the idea in your head that you're too young or too inexperienced. Instead, soak up the opportunities you're experiencing and use them to become a better version of you, whatever that means to you.

Once you accept what you are, the work you produce will be filled with much more confidence and much more value.

Habit 10: Holding Grudges

"I forgot that you existed. It isn't love, it isn't hate, it's just indifference" –
Taylor Swift

Correct me if I'm wrong, but having conflicts with the people in your life brings so many more issues than it's worth.

I hate having conflicts with people.

It makes my stomach twist. It makes my armpits sweat (TMI, sorry but it's true). It makes me nervous to go to places that I shouldn't be nervous about. It adds a whole lot of extra stress to my life than what it's worth.

With that being said, for a long time, I was a very unforgiving person. I never forget the wrongs that are done to me. I can still remember things that were said to me in freaking middle school. I rarely changed my mind about a person once they had done me wrong even if I was 12 when it happened.

I was the self-proclaimed queen of holding grudges. I was a one-strike-your-out type of girl. Spoiler alert: it did not get me very far.

When I was in high school, I had my first ever long-term boyfriend. His name is Richie and at the time, he was the hottest name to go around Howell High School. We started dating the summer after freshman year, all the way throughout sophomore year, and into the fall of junior year. He was the first person I said I love you to and my first real boyfriend. Adorable, I know.

Sophomore year, I sat next to this girl, let's call her Jessica, in Spanish class. I don't know about you guys, but I personally found Spanish class to be quite boring. It was also one of the classes I couldn't take at an advanced level so I was stuck in a class with the imbeciles of Howell High School. Ugh.

To make the time a little more interesting, me and Jessica engaged gossip about what was going on in our life, as most fifteen-year-olds do. She was not an imbecile so I didn't mind the interaction.

At the time, she was in love with this kid who went to our local private school and she would fill me in every Monday about any updates she had on the situation. Similarly, I would fill her in on all the juicy details of my relationship with Richie. By the way, at fifteen there are hardly ever any "juicy" details about a relationship other than you were allowed to be in the house for ten minutes alone without any parents.

Now Jessica and I weren't exactly BFFs, but we knew each other pretty well from mutual friends and got along in class. She always made me smile but telling me how cute my relationship was. "You are Richie are so cute" she would say. "I hope you guys stay together forever" she would say. "You're so lucky" she would say.

When the next fall came, Jessica and I progressed to Spanish III, unfortunately in different classes this time, and I didn't see her around at school as much. Shortly after the start of the new school year, my relationship with Richie came to an end, which was initiated by myself. No hard feelings, it just wasn't working anymore so I walked out the door.

A month and a half later at track practice, someone had broken the news to me that -surprise, surprise - Jessica was Richie's new girlfriend.

His new what?

A month?

My immediate reaction was: I hated this girl.

Who did she think she was? And who did he think he was replacing me so quickly? Doubts about the both of them quickly flooded my brain. Was she lying all the times she said we looked cute together? Did I mean nothing to him during our whole relationship if he could replace me so quickly? Was she trying to sabotage me this whole time? Were they both trying to sabotage me this whole time?

I immediately took my place as the petty ex-girlfriend. Every time I passed Jessica in the hallway I would make sure to put my meanest glare on. My best friend at the time egged me on to compose a nasty tweet, which I don't remember exactly but was something along the lines of "it's really sad to see people downgrade". Yikes. I just cringed admitting that. To make matters worse, Jessica saw the tweet and proceeded to text me asking me if I had a problem with her, which I promptly ignored. Ah, the immaturity of 15-year-olds.

The next time I saw Richie since finding out the news was on the night of our national honor's society induction (note: he didn't go to our school). Jessica's name was before mine alphabetically (because just about everyone is when your last name starts with a W), and when her name was called I heard an all too familiar whoop and holler from the crowd.

Chills ran down my spine as I turned to the left and saw Richie standing up in the auditorium, fists raised in the air, shouting for Jessica. My armpits immediately began to sweat and my face burned.

"Isn't that your ex-boyfriend?" the girl next to me asked. I sheepishly nodded, half in embarrassment and half in anger and jealousy.

That night I went home and hid behind my phone screen, composing yet another nasty tweet. This time I wrote "he doesn't even go here". Yes, I quoted mean girls. No, I am not proud of it. You really shouldn't ever quote mean girls to talk about another person.

The fire quickly rose between Jessica and me as months turned into years that passed by. She and Richie are still together to this day and for a while, every post was a slap in the face to me. I was so sick of getting mad when seeing her face that I simply unfollowed her on social media to avoid getting worked up every time she posted.

Recently, I was having a conversation with a friend who mentioned they had grown up together. After finding out where I went to high school, she asked me if I knew Jessica. At the sound of her name, my smile immediately disappeared.

"Yeah we were friends until she started dating my ex-boyfriend a month after we broke up, junior year in high school," I said. That was always my immediate reaction when someone mentioned her. I wanted them to understand what kind of twisted, evil witch she was.

But after the sentence left my mouth, I thought for a second.

Junior year in high school.

I was 20 years old, getting myself worked up about something that had happened before I was old enough to get my driver's license!

Especially as girls, it's never easy to forget when someone did you wrong. You might "let it go" but it will always be imprinted in your brain. Nothing gets past us girls!

When we're in high school, our world is small. It consists of the people we pass in the hallway every day and then some. When we get to college, our world broadens a little but it's still small. I mean think about it – I go to a university of 37,000 students but there are 7 billion people in this world.

Let me tell you some cold, hard facts sister, things are going to happen. Your ex is going to find a new girlfriend. Your old best friend is going to start hanging out with new people. You're going to run into your freshman year roommate that you didn't get along with at a party. Unless you relocate to Australia, you're probably going to run into people that you've had an issue with.

The world is big, but our worlds are small. You have two ways you can live in it: you can get worked up and profusely sweat when you see someone you dislike, or you can let it go.

Improvement #10: Let Go of Your Grudges

The almighty Taylor Swift once wrote, "I forgot that you existed. It isn't love, it isn't hate, it's just indifference". Those lyrics are one of my top favorites of all time. The thing about Taylor Swift songs (love her or hate her, you have to admit it) is there's a lot of meaning behind them. Well, most of them … that one part in We Are Never Ever Getting Back Together is still debatable.

I think we should all try and get into Taylor's mindset here. You are going to have falling outs with people. You are going to have breakups. You are going to have people who treat you unfairly in your life. Unfortunately, some people are just really crappy and we can't control that. We can pray for them though that they find peace with themselves and learn to be better people.

At that moment a few months ago, I chose to let go of all of my negative feelings towards Jessica and everyone else that I was holding grudges against.

I was the one who initiated my breakup with Richie. Letting someone go means there is a likely possibility they will move on and find someone new and that is something you have to accept and know if you're going through a breakup. Even if I had been the one who was dumped, it was four years ago. Four whole years. Why the heck did I still care?

I'm tired of feeling anxious when someone I dislike walks into the room. I'm tired of worrying about which sorority is mixing with my boyfriend's frat because that girl is in the said sorority and might judge me or make a scene if I show up. Referring back to a few chapters ago, I'm tired of letting other people ruin my happiness and I'm tired of ruining it for other people. No one likes a negative Nancy.

It is much more effort to dislike someone than it is to feel indifferent towards them. I'm not saying to become indifferent to everyone. I'm saying it's better to be indifferent than to hate.

I had a falling out with some of my best friends who I am set to live with in the fall. My friends now ask me if I'm nervous or why I didn't back out of my lease. They wonder how it's going to work and how much tension there will be.

The way I see it, there's only tension if you allow it. There are things they did that were hurtful to me but holding onto that grudge is only going to make for an awkward living space. I can choose to stay mad at them and be adamant against liking them. I can choose to never trust them again. I can also choose to be indifferent, and that is the path I've chosen to take. What happened between us was not on a level so terrible that it's worth feeling uncomfortable in my own home every day.

Everyone messes up and I bet there is a time you did something wrong towards a friend or loved one. None of us are perfect, I've had my fair share of mess-ups and blow-ups. Harnessing those negative feelings is only going to create a negative environment for you.

Ask yourself if the wrong is worth the negative energy that comes with holding a grudge. If your best friend in the whole world sleeps with your boyfriend, that's something that maybe can't be forgotten that easily. But if a girl you were friendly with dates your ex-boyfriend, is it worth getting heated up over?

I wish I could go back and apologize to not only the people I was outwardly negative towards but also myself for creating that negative space to live in. I wish I could erase the tweet drafts I composed four years ago and just let Jessica and Richie be. Unfortunately, I can't but I can choose to face grudges differently going forward.

Remember my roommate Elaina? We've gotten into a few arguments during our time living together. The last time we got into an argument she said to me, "I don't want to be mad at you anymore. It's just too hard and awkward being mad" and I agreed with her whole-heartedly. Instantly, the bad vibes had vanished.

It was a lot of effort having to avoid going downstairs when she was out and about or feeling the tension that filled the room when we were both in it. Negative energy surrounded us and we had both had enough. That's another reason why I love Elaina, she puts her pride aside to make amends and we can all learn from her in that sense.

What grudges are you holding on to? Maybe you're upset because all your friends went out without you on Friday night. Maybe you're feeling bitter because you and your housemate got into a big fight. Maybe your brother called you a, ahem, female dog and you both launched into a screaming match.

Whatever your grudges are, ask yourself if it's worth the negative space you're creating for yourself by holding onto them, and then let them go.

73

CH. 11

Habit #11: Refusing Help

"Venture outside your comfort zone. The rewards are worth it" – Rapunzel, Tangled.

There are two reasons why I love to do things all by myself, like a big girl. The first is that gratifying feeling of accomplishment when you're done. The second is because I'm straight-up lazy.

Holy crap, am I lazy.

I have to set a ton of reminders on my phone to get myself to do simple things like register for a new parking pass online, which I can do from my bed. I know what you're thinking. I get on Instagram every day and motivate people to get up and get moving. I stay true to that and getting up is not my problem. My laziness kicks into action when I have things to do that I don't want to do. For example, when my mom tells me to dust my room. No thank you.

During my freshman year of college, I enrolled in the first statistics class I would ever be taking in my life. No, it was not for fun, it was a business pre-requisite. Mean, median, mode, probability, how hard could it be? I did my research on the ever-trusty Rate My Professor and signed up for Professor Moondra's class. He had a great rating and everyone older than me suggested I take it with him. If I did, I was a shoo-in for an A. It was at 8:10 in the morning on Monday's though, which was the real kicker. I traded my sleep for the high chance of getting an A and pressed register.

When winter break came to its close, I got an email of the syllabus for Stats for Business. It was signed, Professor Zhao.

Professor Zhao?! This must be a mistake! No, you see I signed up for Moondra, not this Zhao lady. I quickly double-checked the course schedule planner for the spring semester and sure enough, where Moondra's name had once been next to Monday 8:10 was now someone named Zhao. This was not the last time the RU Screw had waltzed into my life, but it was the first time I learned that apparently, Rutgers can just change professors on you, days before the semester starts and there's nothing you can do about it.

The first day of class was a disaster. I mean, it was a complete and utter disaster. Not only did this Zhao woman speak less English than my immigrant grandparents did, but she wrote everything on the blackboard in a lecture hall. She must not have been aware that my vision is a negative six in both eyes and that even with contacts in and sitting in the first row, I still wasn't able to see a thing she wrote down.

To make matters worse, it turns out that statistics has a lot more to it than just probability and keeping track of things. The first exam was approaching and I was absolutely, positively screwed. I even read the textbook and I was still screwed. That's when my friend in the class, who was also struggling, asked me if I wanted to go to the tutor with him on Tuesday night. Rutgers offers free group tutoring for many of their classes and they're held at the learning centers on each campus. This tutor happened to be located on the campus I lived on and the learning center was just two buildings over from my dorm.

My immediate reaction was heck no. No, I do not want to go expend the energy it'll take to walk to the tutor in the freezing cold of February in New Jersey. No, I do not want to go through the mental pain of being bored to death by whoever this tutor guy was. My plans for Tuesday night consisted of eating a sub from takeout sub night at the dining hall and then laying down in my bed until the food coma surpassed. I was very, very busy on Tuesday night.

But I was also doomed for my statistics midterm. I wrestled with the idea up until Tuesday night. If I studied hard enough I would probably be fine right? Did I really need this tutor? I mean yeah, I was pretty lost but maybe there will be a curve or something.

Finally, I decided to join my friend on his trip to the learning center. I brought my takeout sub with me, packed my backpack, and headed over with a list of questions. When I got there, I was surprised at how young and cool the tutor was. Everyone in the room was there for different stat classes or different professors and somehow, he was able to help everyone. Kunal is a straight-up wizard and you will never be able to convince me otherwise. God bless that man's soul.

My first session with Kunal was successful, which led me to my second session with Kunal. When I got my first exam grade back, I saw a big 86 on my paper. For someone who was convinced she was destined to fail this class, I was pretty dang proud of an 86! That was when I decided Kunal was in fact a statistics wizard so I returned to the learning center for my third session. Before I knew it, I was going to him two-three times a week to stay on top of what we were learning. When the semester ended, I was more than pleased to see an A on my final transcript.

What would have happened if I never accepted that I needed help? I probably, no I definitely, would have failed that first exam and most likely the other two as well. I would've had a big hole in my GPA and had to retake the course over the summer or next fall.

It seems simple, if you're struggling in school go get a tutor. If your mental health is on edge, go see a therapist. If you can't figure out how to enter someone's order in the tablet at work, go ask your manager. If you can't lift the case of water into your cart at the grocery store, ask the strong man next to you for help.

So why do we so often refrain from asking for help?

Asking for help is often associated with failure or weakness. If you can't lift that case of water on your own, you are physically weak. If you need to go to the writing center to write your essays, you're weak-minded.

Well let me ask you this – the first time you rode a bike, did you have training wheels on? Unless you're some sort of cycling prodigy, you most likely did. Eventually, the training wheels come off and you're able to ride on two wheels but your dad is holding on to the back of your seat. One day he lets go, and you're able to ride all on your own!

In this day and age, women have so much to prove for themselves. We are constantly battling to prove that we can match and exceed men's standards. It's something we shouldn't have to do but it's the reality of our world. Asking for help can be scary when it's associated with weakness. We are constantly trying to show off our capabilities and asking for help seems like a step backward from that.

Asking for help is a big deal for me. I want to be able to control my own life. I want to be able to accomplish things on my own in case I ever am really alone. I have this idea in my head that one day I'm going to live in my own apartment or house and I'm going to need to able to fix things or do things by myself, even if it's as simple as carrying a case of water up a few flights of stairs.

But then I take a step back and remember all of my firsts. The first time I drove a car, I had a driving instructor to help me. The first time I lived by myself, I had my parents to help me move in. The first time I went to an interview, I had my mom drive me. The first time I learned to do a crow pose in yoga, I had Nike Master Trainer Alex Silver-Fagan on my phone screen to help me.

My point is that asking for help is not a sign of weakness. It just means you need guidance.

Improvement #11: Accept and Seek Help When Needed

Seeking help does not mean you're weak.
Seeking help does not mean you've failed.
Seeking help does not mean that you're not good enough.

If I hadn't accepted that I needed help, I would probably have had to fork over my own money to pay to take statistics for business again. Two years later when I took Statistical Methods (the second statistics course that's required for business students), I willingly and openly went back to Kunal almost every week to stay on track. Sometimes I would go and we wouldn't even teach me much, he would just give me practice problems to make sure that I was on the right track.

Getting a tutor does not mean that I am stupid. It doesn't mean that I'm unable to comprehend things alone or that I'm slow-minded. I sought help to stay on track with my work and to have a resource to ask questions so I could excel in my learning. Just as you receive motivational quotes on your apple watch every day or have the "sprinkle of Jesus" app downloaded to help guide you, I went to a tutor to guide me.

Was it a hassle? Yes, it was not enjoyable getting on a smelly, sweaty bus to go to Busch campus every week. Did other people think low of my when I told them I was going to the tutor? No, they didn't. In college, everyone's just looking to get the best GPA they can. Some people try harder than others but it's the end goal for most of us. When I told my housemates I was going to the tutor they looked at me with admiration, inspired by the fact that I was taking steps to better my education instead of laying in my bed watching another episode of How to Get Away with Murder. At the time, I was extremely invested in How to Get Away with Murder.

No one expects you to be perfect the first time you try something. You're probably going to screw up a few times or need guidance the first week of your new job and there is nothing wrong with that as long as you learn from it.

Minutes ago, I messaged my dad's cousin who I haven't talked to in years. We aren't super close but he's a really inspirational person and I know he wrote a book that was a best-seller in sports psychology! I, on the other hand, have no idea how to get this dang thing published. I pushed aside my pride and messaged him asking for help and guidance. He responded saying he would be glad to FaceTime and explain to me how he went about things. You're reading this now so hey, I guess it worked!

The other day I was supposed to move out of my house at school with my dad but at the last minute, he didn't end up coming along. I was crying in my car unsure of how I was going to get this heavy and large dresser out of my room by myself. My mom was unable to help me and my brother was at work. As simple as it would've been if I could have picked the dresser up myself, I am 5"3" and the likeliness of me breaking my spine in the process was high. I texted my friend John and asked him for his help. John is a massive six-foot-something football player at our school who can push cars down the street. That's right, push cars. He was more than happy to help me, heck he even carried the dresser out all by himself!

If I hadn't reached out, the dresser would've been stuck in my bedroom and I would've most likely had a panic attack in the driver's seat of my car.

My inability to move the dresser myself does not make me weak. I like to consider myself pretty strong actually but this dresser was twice my weight and physically I am just too small to carry it myself.

Society puts this pressure on us that we have to do things ourselves. Society tells us that the only person that has your back is you. Society puts all these entrepreneurs or pop stars into the limelight and shows us how they did accomplish their dreams, but seldom did they do it alone. Mark Zuckerberg didn't create Facebook by himself, he had the help of Eduardo Saverin in the beginning and then a whole team to help him run the business.

There is a difference between asking for help and looking for the easy way out. Looking for the easy way out is cheating my friends, and it will only bite you in the booty later on. Asking for help is looking to improve. Asking for help is using your resources wisely to unlock new levels of skills and knowledge. Asking for help is getting an extra hand because yours are already full. Asking for help does not mean your weak. Asking for help does not mean you've failed. Asking for help means you're growing.

CH. 12

Habit #12: Sleeping Too Late

"Early to bed, early to rise, makes a man healthy and wise" – Benjamin Franklin

You can tell a lot about a person by the time they wake up in the morning.

How often do you hear of a college kid who's in bed by 11:30? Probably not too often. I mean, there's homework assignments and club meetings that don't end until ten at night and don't even get me started on the weekends.

I don't know about you guys, but nightlife at Rutgers doesn't light up until about 11 PM. That means arriving at parties fashionably late at 11:30. And then Daniel's Pizza is open practically all night so I might as well get a slice at 2:30 and of course, we have to post-game. Who doesn't post-game? Everything goes down at the post-game. And that guy you like? He doesn't text you until at least 1 AM anyway so you have to wait up to see if he'll come around.

If your first classes of the day don't start until 1:30 PM, you're probably not going to start any work until way after they're done. Plus, there are other things to do like workout and eat and you'll probably get distracted talking to your housemates, and don't forget that chapter starts at 10 PM every Monday.

It's easy to fall into this cycle of stay up late, wake up late, repeat.

Sometimes, it's inevitable to go to sleep later than expected. If your meeting doesn't start at 10, you're not getting home until at least 11 and then you have to wash up, wind down, yadda, yadda.

When I was going through my breakup and all the other crazy things that were happening over winter break, I slept in until 10 AM every day. You might have just gone, psh 10 AM? She thinks that's sleeping in, she has no idea. And if you did, then pay special attention to what I'm saying here.

My days started around 10 AM and I would get up, go through my morning routine, and hit the gym. I wouldn't get back from the gym until about 1 PM and by then I was already tired. Over winter break there's not much to do so I would spend the day being a couch potato and simultaneously being miserable about my life. My reasoning for waking up at 10 was, well, what else is there to do? Each day I brought on (notice how I take responsibility for this because I am in control of my emotions), pain, and misery that filled every waking minute. To minimize the pain, I would just sleep in. If I was unconscious than I wouldn't be able to feel sad.

When night fell, I wasn't tired from sleeping in so late. I would sit in my bed and find a million other things to do. I would scroll through Instagram, binge-watch Netflix, watch YouTube, read, listen to sad music, and cry (which rarely helps by the way). I would finally fall asleep around 1:30 and then do it all over again.

How productive was I during this time?

Zip. Nada. Zero. Not at all. I was not productive in any other sense besides getting to the gym every day and beating over 1000 levels of candy crush, hold your applause thank you.

I am the type of person whose brain shuts off after 10 PM. That's usually my cutoff for productivity and that's when I start to unwind for the day or get the party started if it's Thursday-Saturday. For me, staying up late just means wasting my hours away doing absolutely nothing but draining my phone battery or watching too much Netflix. So when I wake up late the next day, I have less time to be productive and get stuff done.

One of the greatest parts of college is living with your friends and no adults. Although I'm past my dorm-living days, I loved every day of being in my dorm because I was constantly surrounded by friends! My neighbor Sal and I were very close and hung out often, mostly watching Breaking Bad, and down the hall, Mike had a George Foreman grill that he snuck in and we would stay up watching whatever concoction he come up with from stolen dining hall food.

The hours would pass by and before we knew it, it was already 1 AM and we were still hanging out in the third-floor lounge hardly sleepy at all.

For the past two years, I lived with ten girls. All ten of us have different majors and were part of different clubs and teams so our schedules hardly ever matched up. The only time we ever really got to all be together was at night after Elaina got back from the radio, Samara got back from pre-dental society, Macey and Steph got home from dance practice, you get the idea. Since we couldn't hang out until late, we stayed up late. Even after I would retire to bed the other girls would stay up for hours. Half the fun of living with your friends is being able to hang out with them every day,

When I was dating my ex-boyfriend, I often didn't get to see him until around 10-11 PM. Obviously, I wasn't going to trek halfway across campus to waltz in and say goodnight so we would stay up until the wee hours of the morning. When the sunlight peeked through the window the next morning, I would bury myself deeper into the covers and fall back asleep. I loved spending time with him and waking up meant that it was time to leave, plus I was tired from staying up late, so I resulted in falling back asleep later and later.

What I'm trying to prove here is that I get it. No one expects you to be in bed by 12 on the weekends. Losing time is easy and before we know it, we're in this cycle of sleeping in and staying up late and hitting the snooze button seven times before we actually get up. But like everything in life, there needs to be a balance.

Improvement #12: Make it a Goal to Get up By Nine

You think I'm crazy right now. I know you do. Before I explain, let me say that no one expects you to get up at 9 AM after partying all night so Saturday and Sunday are exempt from this rule. But, you should still make an effort to get up these days. Just because it's the weekend doesn't mean you can stay in bed all day sister!

There are 24 hours in a day. The earlier you get up, the more time you have to get things done. Be honest, out of all the times you've stayed up until 2 AM, how many times were you studying or working or exercising at that hour? Probably zero times, maybe once or twice before an exam. But you just said half the fun of living with friends is hanging out with them every day and I can only hang out with my friends after 11 – you're right, I did say that. But I also said there needs to be a balance. Here are a few tips to help you create this balance and to avoid falling into a whacky sleep schedule cycle.

Start doing your homework throughout the day

I talked about this a little before, but doing homework throughout the day will reduce the amount of homework you need to do at night. If you're finished with your homework early, then you have time to hang out earlier! I like to do my homework in the time I have in between classes. This leaves me less work to do after classes are over and when my brain stops working at 10 PM, I'm ready to relax and hang out with my housemates for an hour or so and I don't feel guilty about having homework and studying looming over me.

Know when you have time to hang out and when you don't

The older we get, the more responsibilities we have. Every Monday of my junior year I had a club meeting and then an e-board meeting afterward. When I came home around 10:30, my housemates were all in the living room watching TV and hanging out. As much as I would've loved to join them, I said my hello's and went upstairs to unwind. It sucks not being able to join them but I know that tomorrow night I don't have a club meeting so I can hang out with them then! The same goes for the midterm season. If you have a big chemistry midterm on Wednesday, you'll have to pass on the lounge hangout session going on in your dorm and get yourself to bed. The midterm will be over tomorrow so you can hang out with everyone then! Some days you'll have a boatload of time to spare and some days you'll need to be the adult you are and remind yourself of the priority list you made.

Turn on your screen-time limits

Hear me out – now I'm not too sure about Androids, but iPhones can shut off your accessibility to apps after a certain time. I set my phone to shut off-screen time at 12:30 AM during weekdays. Most of the time I go to bed late is because I'm sitting on TikTok for hours in bed. It's something I'm not proud of, but I do it. Turning on your screen time limits is your phone's way of telling you, get to bed girl, you're spending way too much time here!

As I mentioned before, I like to map out my days. It helps to ease my anxiety so I don't feel so overwhelmed. This past semester, my earliest class was at noon. I could've slept in and spent the morning doing whatever I wanted but instead, I made it part of my routine to be in the gym by 9 every day. This gave me enough time to work out, come home and shower, and have a snack before leaving for class. It also knocked my workout out of the way so I could spend my afternoon doing homework instead of worrying that I still have to get to the gym. Planning early activities helps me get my butt out of my warm bed and kickstart my day.

Are there going to be days where you just need an extra hour of sleep? Yes. Are there going to be days where you don't hear your alarm? Yes. You're going to mess up with anything you do. It's the effort of creating the habit that counts. The same goes for diet - there are going to be days where you have a few cookies and mess up your clean eating and that is okay, as long as it's not every day that you're having those mess-ups.

At least try. If not for now, then for your future self. One day you're going to graduate and get a job. You might even have one lined up now, or at least an internship. Most of the time, these jobs are going to require you to be working by 9 AM which means you'll have to get up. Creating the habit of getting up at a decent time now will only leave you better prepared for when that day comes.

As I said, you can tell a lot about a person by the time they wake up. You have two choices every day, you can get out of bed and make the most of your day or you can watch it pass by from under your covers. Goals won't be met if we spend our days sleeping. So, when your alarm starts ringing tomorrow at 8:30, it's time to wake up.

ABOUT THE AUTHOR

Liz Wei is a NASM certified personal trainer and current Rutgers student, majoring in Marketing. This is her debut as a published author! She can be found on Instagram @liftswithliz